SAFE DISTANCE SAVE LIVES

Mallika Sothinathan

Copyright © 2021 Mallika Sothinathan.

All rights reserved. No part of this book may be used or reproduced by any means, graphic, electronic, or mechanical, including photocopying, recording, taping or by any information storage retrieval system without the written permission of the author except in the case of brief quotations embodied in critical articles and reviews.

Balboa Press books may be ordered through booksellers or by contacting:

Balboa Press
A Division of Hay House
1663 Liberty Drive
Bloomington, IN 47403
www.balboapress.com
844-682-1282

Because of the dynamic nature of the Internet, any web addresses or links contained in this book may have changed since publication and may no longer be valid. The views expressed in this work are solely those of the author and do not necessarily reflect the views of the publisher, and the publisher hereby disclaims any responsibility for them.

Any people depicted in stock imagery provided by Getty Images are models, and such images are being used for illustrative purposes only.
Certain stock imagery © Getty Images.

ISBN: 978-1-9822-6474-1 (sc)
ISBN: 978-1-9822-6476-5 (hc)
ISBN: 978-1-9822-6475-8 (e)

Library of Congress Control Number: 2021903864

Print information available on the last page.

Balboa Press rev. date: 03/12/2021

Contents

Introduction 1

Mallika Bakshi Sothinathan 3

Foreword 5

Shirin Ariff 7

Abdullah Zakaria 11

Sujay Jha 13

Sandeep Bose 15

Shelley Jarrett 17

Seemant Kumar Singh 19

Meeta Khanna 21

Roger Caesar 25

Lata Gullapalli 29

Karan Sehmbi 31

Steve Elliot 35

Hari Iyer 37

Melanie Pereira 39

Cheryl Jairaj 41

Aditya Seth 43

Ranjan Bakshi 45

Sean D Actor 49

Asis Sethi 53

Dean Boye 57

Jay Wijesundara 59

    Episode 34 - Power Within - Inspiring stories of women entrepreneurs 60

Ujjwal Roy Chowdhuri alias Ricky 65

    Episode -18 The Protest 2020 66

Episode - 38 - Mental Health Awareness and Wellness Workshop - Part 1 71

Episode - 39 - Mental Health Awareness and Wellness Workshop - Part 2 77

Editor's Biography 85

Co- Author's Biography 85

References 87

Authors 89

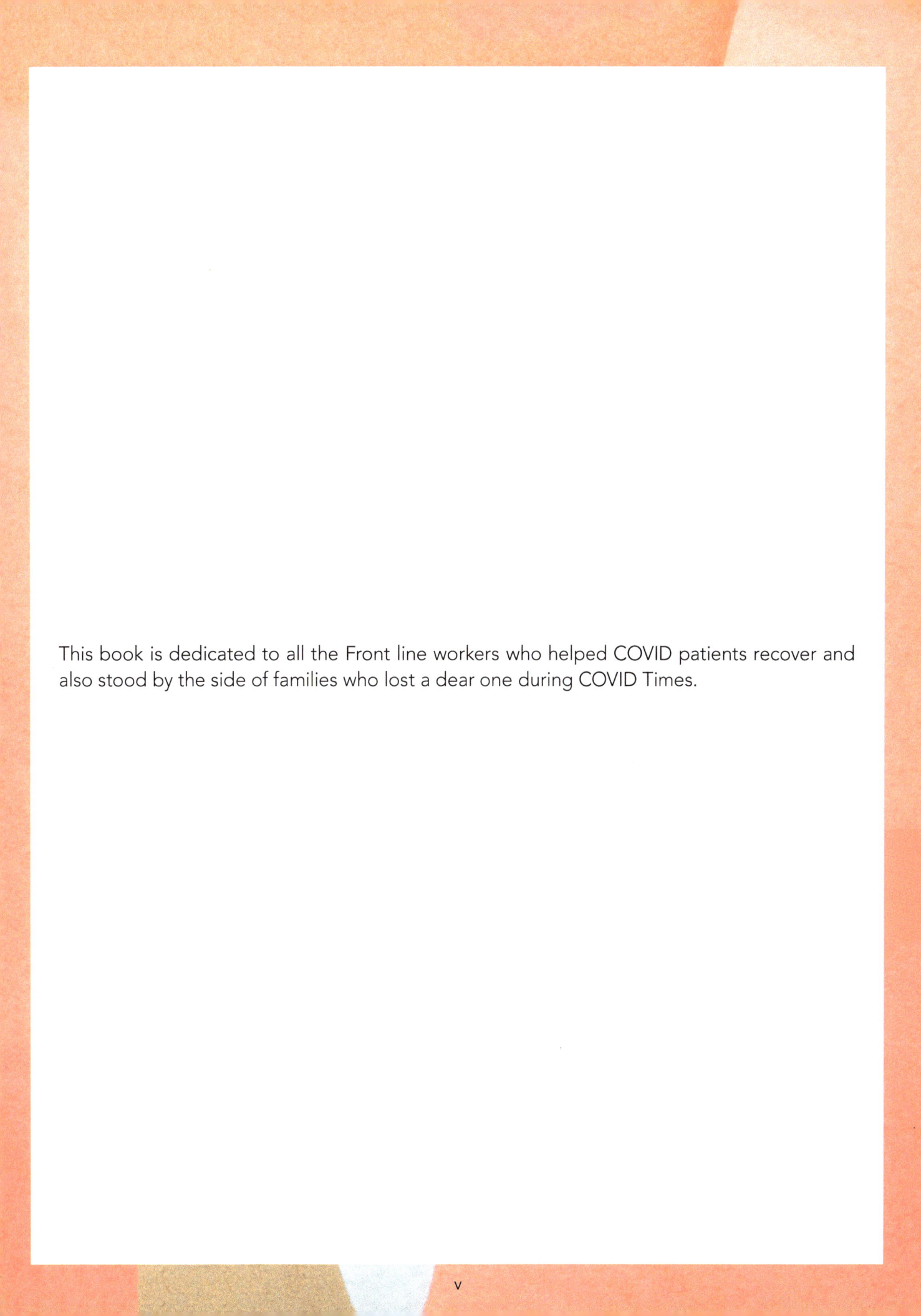

This book is dedicated to all the Front line workers who helped COVID patients recover and also stood by the side of families who lost a dear one during COVID Times.

Introduction

It is a delightful day to share this special journey with all of you. This journey began during the first phase of COVID-19 pandemic. When the world suddenly stopped, my brother and I had to travel for our beloved family members and especially our dad, baba as we lovingly called him. Baba had taught me never to give up and always strive for excellence but through good service to others. He said it is important to make progress but never at the cost of others. COVID-19 has just taught us to be humble. So, the series started in the closed room for 14 days in my bedroom and I started talking to my friends and family via zoom and thus began the series Safe Distance Save Lives. I did not have the adequate equipment (camera), but I had the support of like-minded people who were equally eager to share the stories and so the journey began. Initially the plan was to do 8 minute interviews twice a week, which changed to half hour programs with some heated discussions and valuable content. It was indeed sometimes very surprising to learn about resources and find so much in common with them. The aim of this program was to start a conversation. Get people to talk and discuss the issues that would have stayed behind the doors. We engaged in meaningful discussions about the Black Lives Matter Protest, rise in mental health issues, the impact of COVID-19 on a variety of industries including the entertainment industry, and experiences of the front-line workers. I thoroughly enjoyed this journey and hope you do too through this book. The stories are based on the episodes/interviews that were aired on our Youtube Channel.

Sincerely,

Mallika Sothinathan

 **SAFE DISTANCE SAVE LIVES**

MALLIKA

Mallika Bakshi Sothinathan

Background

Mallika is the Director of New Horizon Media Arts. After obtaining a master's in mass communication from Mass Communication Research Center Delhi, she worked in the Indian TV industry with channels like Zee and ETV. Mallika migrated to Canada in 1999 and became a Canadian citizen but still maintained a deep connection to India. After working 19 years in retail, Mallika gained a wide range of experience including 7 years of operation management and 12 years in planogram, data design, and analytics.

In 2017, Mallika returned to media production. With her fluency in four South Asian languages, she completed a feature-length documentary on the domestic workers of India called "Crossing the River of Life". The film touches on their daily struggle, violence, human trafficking, and empowerment. Working on the film inspired Mallika to become more involved as an activist in advocating for women and children's rights. Thereafter she produced another documentary released September 2020"Sree Dancing Through the Seasons." Thereafter produced "Safe Distance Save Lives", a web series. Recently she launched "Let's Talk" with Ekta Wadhwa. She is a Toastmaster and a Social Worker. She is currently a corporate executive and a Customer Success manager in a prestigious IT company.

Foreword

Enclosed within the covers of this book is a time capsule of the first few months of the strangest times of our lives. Who would have thought that a microscopic virus would have such a macroscopic, world-changing impact in such a tech-advanced time of our lives!

No matter who we are, what we do, where we live, we are reckoned by our helplessness and fragility. Along with physical health and life- threatening risks, the global pandemic has impacted our mental, emotional and economic health. This was 2020 for us.

Beyond Black Lives Matter and US President Trump, Covid-19 continues to dominate world news. We have new words in our vocabulary-social distancing, quarantine, flatten the curve, six feet apart, zoom calls, second wave, covid-fatigued and "speak moistly". Toilet paper, masks and hand-sanitizers have become part of our survival kits. No one really knows better, and we need each other now, more than ever.

The 30 stories in this book are relatable and shared experiences of many. As you read them, you will feel comfort and consolation in the reassurance that you are not alone. That we are in this together. Perhaps sharing our stories is one way of dealing with despair and saving lives while we keep safe distance.

# SAFE DISTANCE SAVE LIVES

SHIRIN ARIFF

Shirin Ariff

Background

Shirin Ariff is a 5 times international best-selling and award-winning author, an international speaker and Resiliency Coach. She has survived Cancer. Shirin's coaching program **Be Your Own North Star** is for people who are feeling stuck and can find freedom and self-governance to navigate through their lives. Shirin has two degrees from the University of Calcutta with majors in English and Education and a minor in Psychology. Shirin holds an Ontario Certified Teacher (OCT) License in Canada. In this episode, she shares her experiences during the COVID-19 lockdown and the actions she has been taking to remain positive and safe.

Episode 3

As a single mother of 4, the experience of this lockdown has been quite a roller-coaster ride for my family. It has been challenging to keep my 3 out of 4 school-going children indoors 24 hours a day, 7 days a week since the lockdown was announced in March 2020. In addition, we have had to cancel a planned family vacation scheduled for the March School Break.

I am trying to keep the experience real for the children by consciously balancing my response to the challenges and opportunities that the lockdown has brought on. I try not to complain in front of the children and focus instead on enabling them to be aware of what's going on in the world around them so we can all do our part with patience.

However, there are days when I experience breakdowns and show my vulnerability. When this happens, I share openly the impact on me and the fact that every day is not the same. This enables the kids to do the same and not be afraid to show their vulnerability. I hold the safe space for them so that they are able to relate with their fears and apprehensions of these unprecedented and unforeseen times. This way, we are able to find that authentic connection and ways to stay positive and grounded because we are in this together.

On a positive note, I see the silver lining and believe that online schooling is a blessing in disguise, as it does not look likely that the children will return to in school learning until September.

Children perform well when they have a routine to follow and that has been disrupted during the lockdown. There are no play dates, extra activities or opportunities for outdoor play. Thankfully, online schooling has made it possible for students to have real-time classes which brings the whole class together and allows them to interact and remain connected with their teachers and peers. This is comforting for the children and brings some amount of normalcy to their lives when everything else has been totally disrupted. Teachers are doing a great job in adapting to the new norm.

We have been hearing the term *social* distancing for a while now. In my mind, I would not call it *social* distancing, because we are still socially connected. I would say, it's more physical distancing. In my understanding, there is a difference in the two terms. I am a people's person and love being with others. Self-isolation can be very tough on a person's mental and emotional well-being and to me, making a heart connect is important. I see this as an opportunity to be more thoughtful about our relationships at a time when we are being asked to maintain physical distancing.

As a speaker and coach, I am used to connecting face to face with people. Due to the lockdown, everything has shifted to a virtual platform and hence there is a need to learn and adapt. Adapting quickly is the key to survival now. This is a profound lesson that we are learning from a live organism, tinier than a roach. In a world where dinosaurs disappeared from the face of this planet, roaches have survived and remained from Jurassic times only because they have a tremendous capacity to adapt. So real or virtual, we have to still make that connection with people. No man is an island they say, we thrive as social beings.

This is truly a time to reflect on how much we take things for granted, especially those things that are freely available to us such as the outdoors. It's time to be grateful for all the good things around us that we so miss now. At the same time, I am aware of what people are dealing with, mentally and emotionally and truly believe that we will stay strong and together as we find a way to cope with this experience.

My message to everyone is to be kind to themselves. It is a very challenging time right now, and if you are dealing with grief, loneliness, fear, you are not alone because this is a global pandemic and people everywhere in the world are going through similar emotions. Don't be afraid or hesitant to reach out and ask for help when you need it. Be kind to yourself, allow some downtime, and practice mind calming techniques such as yoga, meditation or journaling. Nurture and nourish yourself and focus on your well-being.

This episode took place on April 25th, 2020 on New Horizon Media Arts YouTube Channel

SAFE DISTANCE SAVE LIVES

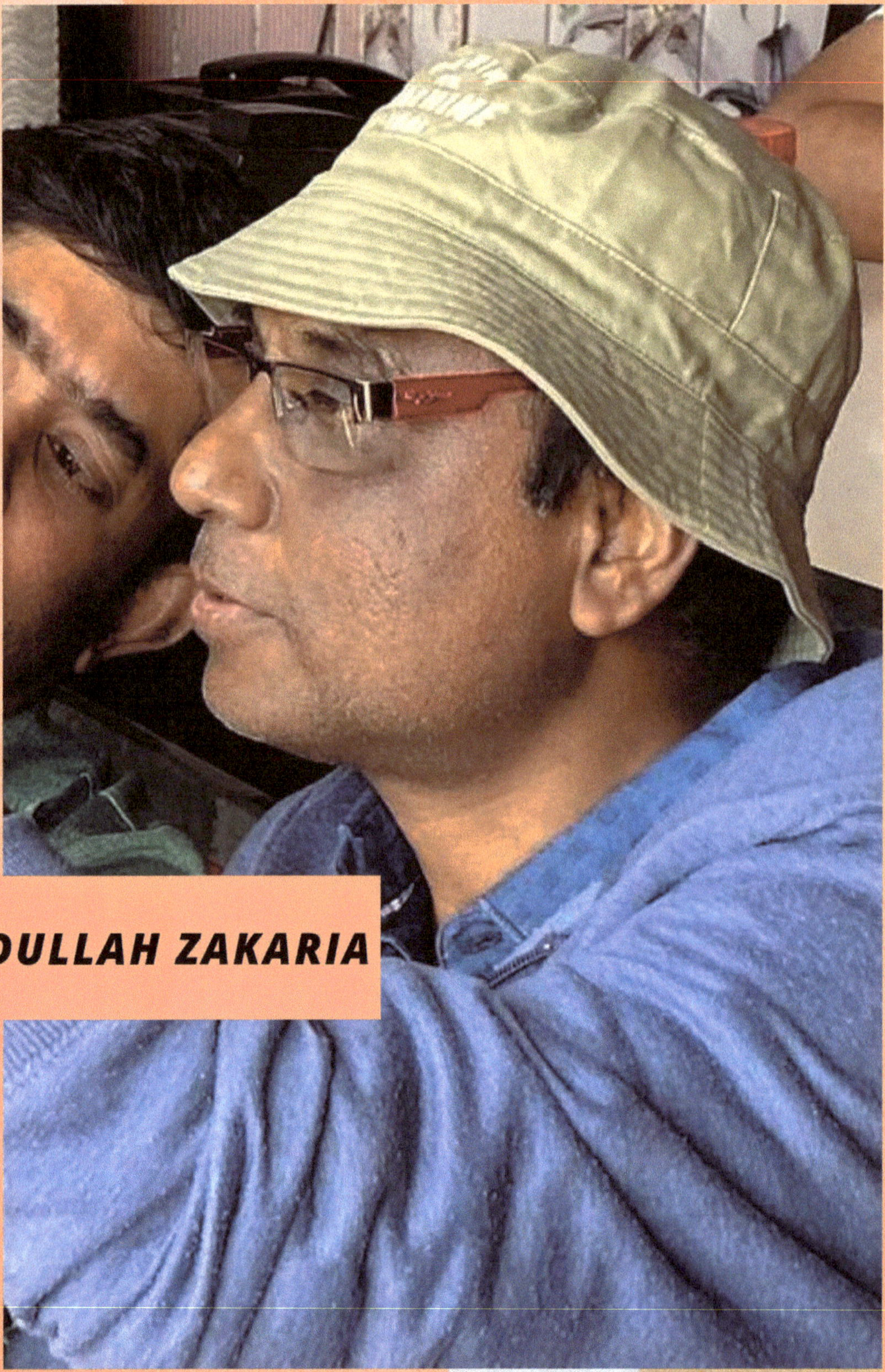

ABDULLAH ZAKARIA

Abdullah Zakaria

Background

Abdullah is an ace Cinematographer, with a long tenure with NDTV, an eminent Indian TV Channel. Abdullah is an alumni of the MCRC, Jamia Millia Islamia, India.

Episode 5

As India begins to lift the lockdown, I would like to reflect on some of the facts in relation to the stringent rules during the lockdown. When the government initially announced a 24/7 lockdown, the number of COVID-19 cases were relatively low. However, now as the lockdown is being lifted and businesses and institutions are reopening, there has been a drastic surge in the number of cases to over a million.

The strongest supporters of the lockdown claim that if this lockdown had not been implemented in March, the cases would have reached over 50 million by now. This argument sounds logical but there is no data readily available to establish this as a fact. On the contrary, some of the experts are skeptical and feel that by December 2020, 70% of the population could be infected, as the situation has escalated and reached its peak. In fact, experts say that about 90% of the people won't even know whether they are infected.

The second argument is that the government needed time to prepare for the outbreak as there weren't enough beds, ventilators, and protective equipment in hospitals. This was an important consideration as India does not produce this equipment, especially the ventilators. Additionally, although two of India's most prominent cities have excellent health care systems, they do not have adequate hospital beds available to treat large numbers of people likely to be impacted by the pandemic.

The lockdown has also seriously impacted the Indian economy. It is highly likely that the GDP ratio and growth rate will drastically drop. Not only were migrant workers affected, but it has also impacted the middle-class population. I work as a freelancer and given the current scenario; I am not doing any better than the migrant laborers. I have been home for the past 3 months with no projects in hand and with no hope for any to come my way in the near future.

To conclude, this lockdown situation has been and continues to be very difficult. There are many countries that have managed to deal with this pandemic much better with partial lockdowns versus imposing a complete lockdown.

This episode took place May 2nd, 2020 on New Horizon Media Arts YouTube Channel

# SAFE DISTANCE SAVE LIVES

SUJAY JHA

Sujay Jha

Background

Sujay Jha is the Director and Chief Executive of Hari Bhari Recyclable Private Limited in India. He has worked for over 40 local bodies, managed waste for all the major cities in India and has been one of the major forces in the waste management industry in India. A quintessential entrepreneur who loves working on disruptive ideas across the globe, he has also founded a supply chain company called FreightNXT along with a few college mates from IIT. A maverick in his qualifications Sujay has legal and management degrees from premium educational institutions. He has worked for over 18 years in companies like Mahindra & Mahindra (Mahindra Logistics Ltd), Xerox Corporation and Tata Teleservices Ltd. He is a focused, result- oriented professional with rich experience in Profit Centre Management, Strategic Planning, Sales & Marketing, Business Development, Key Account Management and Client Relationship Management across various industries.

Episode 8

As a professional in the environment and waste management industry in India, we have plants in *Allahabad* and *Moradabad* that conduct complete integrated solid waste management. As these are a part of essential services in India, they have continued working even during the lockdown. However, there have been a number of changes in the workplace environment and a lot of precautions have to be now taken given the nature of the work. Our team has been providing door-to door services across *Allahabad* and *Moradabad* and the need for protection has increased for junk and scrap dealers as well. In addition, there is a mandate for maintaining more distance and less physical interaction at work.

We have experienced a significant reduction in the amount of waste collected overall, as the shops and businesses are closed due to the lockdown. The waste that is being collected is from households and residences only. During the process, there is a point where the waste is collected and brought to the plant. In the plant, a roster system has been established, whereby only a limited number of people work at any given time to maintain physical distancing. The mass exodus of migrant workers as a result of COVID-19 will have a huge impact on our industry. This exodus will lead to corporations cutting down production, which in turn will result in less waste. We too have been impacted by this. Initially, we were manufacturing 3000 tons of compost which has now been significantly reduced. The greatest impact has been on the subalterns, the junk and scrap dealers and other workers.

On the personal front, my family has been impacted too by the COVID-19 crisis and the lockdown. My wife who is a lawyer has been working from home as the courts are closed and my son, who is in high school is suddenly finding himself in a difficult situation and is struggling the most.

My message to everyone is to be positive. There are many challenges that we are all facing. Our routines have been disrupted as we are all in quarantine. Most importantly, I believe that we should connect closely with our family in order to reduce the overall anxiety and stress.

This episode took place on May 12th, 2020 on New Horizon Media Arts YouTube Channel

SAFE DISTANCE SAVE LIVES

SANDEEP BOSE

Sandeep Bose

Background

Sandeep Bose is an Indian actor and casting director, best known for his role in popular Bollywood films-Dabangg 3 (2019), The Burning Love (2017) and Phantom (2018).

Episode 10

Personally, my life has been affected by the pandemic. As the Prime Minister of India suddenly announced the lockdown effective from March 22, 2020, the shootings of a web series and two films that I had planned for this period had to be cancelled without further notice. In all the global pandemic has significantly affected the entertainment industry in Bollywood.

The film industry employs thousands migrants from all parts of India to perform labor work. This lockdown caused a major crisis for these workers as they lost jobs due to cancelled shoots, were impacted financially and could not go back to their hometowns. However permanent workers like cameramen, light boys etc., who have been working in the film industry for a long time, have survived. They are in a better situation than the daily wage workers, as they have their homes in Mumbai as opposed to the laborers from remote towns.

We are all in this together as many developed countries have failed to control the spread of the virus, thereby adversely impacting the Global Economy. Several members of the Bollywood industry are taking the initiative to spread awareness and encourage people to follow the rules and advice of the government and other experts. Eminent actor Amitabh Bachchan along with other actors created a video to emphasize the importance of staying at home, wearing masks and sanitizing during lockdown. This video encouraged other members as well to create a motivational song titled "Jitega India" to educate and motivate the masses.

While I believe in what Bill Gates has said about the pandemic in calling it a global health crisis I also think that this is a punishment from God to mankind for destroying, polluting, and exploiting nature. Consequently, it is important to have faith and pray, while also taking the necessary precautions to stay safe. We must be aware that COVID-19 will treat everyone equally regardless of religion and race, and people of any social status (rich or poor), and any profession can be impacted. This is a learning experience to respect one another and most importantly nature.

This episode took place on May 19th, 2020 on New Horizon Media Arts YouTube Channel

SAFE DISTANCE SAVE LIVES

SHELLEY JARRETT

Shelley Jarrett

Background

Shelley Jarrett is a multiple award winning Entrepreneur, Magazine Publisher, Speaker, Mentor, and Documentary Film Producer. She started her image consulting business in 2012. The primary objective was to help women dress for success in the workplace. She has been able to accomplish this through workshops, networking conferences, and speaking engagements.

About eight years after forming SJ Image Creations, she merged to a media platform, where she launched an online magazine focusing on image lifestyle and business. She was able to take advantage of various marketing strategies, partnerships and collaborations using other networks to broaden her brand and consumer base.

She has won numerous media and business awards and is committed to telling stories of ordinary people doing extraordinary things. It gives her immense joy to share her experiences, skills, passion and insight on women's issues focusing on gender-based violence and women entrepreneurship.

Episode 11

As I reflect on these past five months, all I can remember is Friday, the 13th of March when we came back home, after screening the final version of our documentary, W'AT ABOWT US in Ottawa, Ontario. In less than 48 hours, the country was moving into lockdown.

We cancelled our spring edition of SMJ Magazine. Although we had thought about publishing an anniversary issue, we had to cancel this as well as death tolls were alarmingly on the rise worldwide, things were looking grimmer and darker, and we were still in lockdown at the beginning of June.

During this period, I have continued to support my community. All through my career, my goal has been to assist women in finding their true selves, to gain self-confidence and be a force in whatever they choose to do. I am part of a women's support group that provides services to women who are victims of domestic violence and are trapped at home with their abusers. As a result of the lockdown, our meetings have become virtual and continue to take place on a weekly basis so timely help, support and resources can be provided to survivors to help them get through these very trying times.

I was spiritually inspired to return to the entrepreneurial course that I had finished in 2012. I could not revert to who I was 8 years ago because of the way I was transformed. I translated my transformation into an e-course for today's women, and it is called **SHIFTNOW**. There has never been such a shift in the world with a whole new vocabulary that is part of our everyday speech: *self-isolation, social distancing, washing hands, deep cleaning, PPE* to name a few. I can't wait to hear *Congratulations* added to the list; the world is COVID-19 free!!

This episode took place on May 23rd, 2020 on New Horizon Media Arts YouTube Channel

SAFE DISTANCE SAVE LIVES

SEEMANT KUMAR SINGH

Seemant Kumar Singh

Background

He is an Inspector General of Police (western range) with its headquarters in the city. Singh had earlier served in *Dakshina Kannada* district in the capacity of Superintendent of Police and then as the first Police Commissioner of the City Police Commissionerate when it was formed. In this episode, he discusses his role in helping India combat the COVID-19 crisis.

Episode 14

Personally, COVID-19 has affected my life but we are taking it in a positive way. My family is staying at home as per the rules of the lockdown, whereas my job falls under the essential services category. Finding a work-life balance during the lockdown has been very difficult for me, as I have to fulfill my duty of serving the country. My family supports me as they realize this and I also try my best to be with them and ensure that I don't interfere with their daily routines at the same time.

There have been radical changes in India as a result of the outbreak of COVID-19. Every police officer, corporation member, and health worker is working tirelessly to combat this pandemic. Under these extenuating circumstances, we have also been compelled to help provide essential groceries to more than 55,000 migrant workers. This initiative was made possible through a team effort of the entire police department.

I would like to share an incident that inspired me to help people who were dealing with hunger in India. As you may know, police phone numbers are available to the public to report a crime or seek help from us. Once, I gave my personal phone number to a few workers, who then gave it out to others and ultimately it got into the hands of the media and got published in the newspapers. After this, I started receiving numerous calls from migrant workers who had either lost their jobs or were struggling to move back to their hometowns due to lack of communication. As I took these calls, I realized the importance and need for helping people in distress.

There are two issues in India that led to the migrant crisis namely the economic downturn and negative social impact. As the literacy rate is very low amongst migrant workers, they are unable to follow the protocol to receive essential grocery items. This has made it difficult for us as we have to deliver the grocery items individually to each person's location.

To some extent my duties at work have changed, as we are doing more social work than before. My daily routine too has changed as I have to now not only take care of my family and help them get through these unprecedented times but also have to sanitize my house and car at all times. This has now become a part of our daily routine, as we have to ensure safety and decrease the spread of the virus.

My message to everyone is that we have to live with it for now. The best way to combat this crisis is to follow the advice of the government- sanitize, stay clean and maintain social distancing.

This episode took place on July 2nd, 2020 on New Horizon Media Arts YouTube Channel

SAFE DISTANCE SAVE LIVES

MEETA KHANNA

Meeta Khanna

Background

Meeta is an artist, who has worked on two ghazals Khushboo' & 'Hasratein, and released Videos on youtube. Ghazals on gaana.com. She has performed ghazals in Punjabi music concerts in several cities including- Chandigarh, Panchkula, and Mohali. Currently, she's the host of a live talk show at Hamdard TV, Brampton, Canada once a week called 'Andaaz Apna Apna.

Episode 19

The term 'lockdown' suddenly came into existence from nowhere! We have seen its usage in times of social disturbances but being used for our safety and wellbeing is certainly ironic. Nonetheless, we are all making a great effort to follow it with utmost seriousness and sincerity.

Humans as a race, are supposed to be the most evolved form of the animal kingdom. We have a highly developed brain that helps us think and analyze things before making decisions. We have the heart to feel things and have various emotions. Our physical and etheric bodies are developed systematically. Our senses are very strong and developed. We are blessed with spirituality through which we can connect with the divine. We need to make use of this incarnation to attain the purpose of our lives by being nice to each other and refraining from causing harm to anyone or anything on Earth.

When I was traveling in the first week of March and reached Canada from India on the 9th of March 2020, I never realized how people would be reacting to this lockdown. Since visiting anyone was not an option available, communication was possible through phone only. Whoever I talked to spoke of things like home arrest, confinement, getting bored, life without shopping, movies being dreadful, uncertainty, question marks, etc. There wasn't even a single positive comment. More so, we seemed so worried about keeping ourselves safe that we would be hesitant to meet our relatives in order to not get infected.

Then came the second phase where people around me started talking about being religious, catching up with prayers, living without shopping, family bonding, following creative pursuits, and of course cooking. It appeared as though we were finally realizing the importance of maintaining good health in natural ways, the blessings of nature, and the blissful resources bestowed upon us by the Divine. We started reading again, thinking, feeling, speaking good for all.

Now we are at a stage where this lockdown is almost ending. And we're going back to work, to our household chores, to stepping out for regular groceries, and catching up with friends. But the risk of a second wave is still out there. We see visuals of people crowding in parks, beaches and partying. It's not that we should stop having fun in life but let us keep our lessons in mind. Let us love and respect our Mother Nature more than ever and let us keep our family bonds stronger with better understanding and harmony in our relationships.

For me, this period turned out to be productive, positive, and full of opportunities. I joined the course "Rhetoric- the Art of Public Speaking", by Harvard University. I started my own blog, caught up on my *riaz* (being a singer), observed discipline in meditation routines, caught up on some long-pending reading, and wrote poetry. My Friday evenings are devoted to the weekly meetings of the esteemed NGO called "Malton Women Council"; where thought- provoking discussions are held on some very important social issues. Apart from participating in virtual meetings of various literary organizations, I have been a part of 3 big virtual concerts that pay tribute to well-known Punjabi poet Shiv Kumar Batalvi, great ghazal singer duo of Late Jagjit Singh and Chitra Singh and the Nightingale of Punjab, Surinder Kaur. I've begun my own show called *Andaaz Apna Apna on Hamdard TV* Channel. There is so much more in life about which I am very excited. So, the lockdown has turned out to be a bliss for some and a lesson for others. Yet, some people prefer to remain aloof and unconcerned about humanity.

This episode took place on July 16th, 2020 on New Horizon Media Arts YouTube Channel

SAFE DISTANCE SAVE LIVES

ROGER CAESAR

Roger Caesar

Background

Roger Caesar is a 4 times Speech Champion. A 3 times International award winning speaker and a 3x semifinalist at the World Championships of Public Speaking. He has spoken at TEDx, MoMondays, Speaker Slam, Fearless Voices and Brampton Mastermind. His dynamic and charismatic style has taken him to many places including Jamaica, California, Boston and New York City. Roger Caesar is the proud owner and president of Caesar Transport Inc., a family owned logistics company servicing the GTA since 1984. His family's main goal has been to provide the best and most reliable delivery services for their customers. They help make your business more efficient and profitable. With over 35 years of experience they deliver your products in perfect condition on time. This allows you to feel relaxed and confident with your shipments so your clients are happy and your business needs are met. With a degree in Marketing and Accounting and over 16 years of experience in Logistics, Roger continues to develop and implement new ideas to further the growth of Caesar Transport Inc. He has dedicated his time to his community and to youth leadership programs. He continues to contribute to Sick Kids Hospital and Knights Table food bank in Brampton. Roger is a motivational speaker who helps others to develop their speaking skills and maximize their potential.

Episode 20

I began my journey in public speaking through Toastmasters, which is known to be a proven gateway for success. I joined Toastmasters to get better at communicating with executives in my company and soon realized that it offered so much more in terms of learning, understanding the value of communication and leadership. As I quickly progressed with getting better at public speaking, I began enrolling in competitions and gradually made my way to becoming a 4x champion!

Prior to COVID-19, I really enjoyed going out to different places, meeting new people and getting to inspire different individuals. This lockdown experience has been unbelievable as it is so different from what we are used to. Personally, I've been spending a lot of time with my kids, as they are at home. It's been very difficult for them, but they are adjusting and learning to deal with it. I think one of the best things I've been able to do is to get connected with other families.

Today, it's very important for everyone to stay informed of the events going on especially related to COVID-19. The same way it is important for me to stay updated and aware about the road closures and local traffic in order to get work done. In the beginning it was easy for my team to get around as the roads were quite smooth. However, despite the changes happening right now due to the pandemic, they are well equipped and are also following all the safety measures at work. We are making sure that the drivers are safe when they go to different places. I've witnessed companies that we deliver to, are following these measures to maintain safety. It's an all-around effort that we are making to work safely.

One word that I would like to use to send a message and give strength to everyone is "matter". You should contribute in some way to improve the lives of people that matter, given the situation we are in. It can be as simple as helping the elderly or sending food to people who need it and for whom it matters.

This episode took place on July 20th, 2020 on New Horizon Media Arts YouTube Channel

SAFE DISTANCE SAVE LIVES

LATA GULLAPALLI

Lata Gullapalli

Background

Lata Gullapalli is an Investment Banker who specializes in Mergers and Acquisitions and is also an Independent Finance Consultant in London. Her passion is to help people. Lata says, "We are like contributors to the subcontractors for the contractors".

Episode 21

In the weeks before the end of the school term, it was easy enough to prepare for Easter break. Schools were to close, and we were off to Poland for the annual fencing competition. The news about COVID-19 in China was announced, but people were not taking it seriously, as it had only spread in one country. However, in a very short time the situation escalated and led to the Mobile World Congress getting cancelled in February of 2020.

This was when we ordered our first set of masks as it was the beginning of a pandemic. As the lockdown in London was announced, people began to stock up on food, schools started closing and our Easter break became indefinite until further notice.

Those were very difficult times for us. Hospitals struggled to manage the overload of COVID-19 cases and were in need of full PPE kits as the virus was highly contagious and spreading rapidly. We did not know what to do with ourselves at home all day. It was to remain calm sometimes. I felt seriously sick and became very weak in the days that followed. We had to think straight and pull ourselves out of this feeling of being overwhelmed.

The first thing we stopped was watching the news all the time, as it only provided information about the rapidly increasing number of COVID cases. There was not enough information on what causes the disease and how it can be treated. To stay productive whilst at home, I signed up for online courses, music sessions and watched some amazing videos of Christmas lectures at the Royal Institution. In addition, I got involved in community services, volunteered to make visors, stitch surgical gowns, prepare and send food (snacks) to hospitals to help their staff. This was very helpful and beneficial for them especially in the beginning, as some hospitals were not organized and equipped to cater food to the staff and frontline workers who were expected to be at work for long hours.

Change in life is normal and actually good for one. While the initial weeks were calm with everyone following the lockdown rules and going out only to get essentials, soon people began to ignore the rules and started to take everything for granted. People started having house parties, visiting each other, and going outdoors without following the government rules of wearing masks or sanitizing. Despite knowing that this virus is extremely contagious and may cause people to die or have diseases, people ignored all the rules.

Honestly, I'm afraid of getting infected, and really urge people to protect themselves and others. We should think about the frontline workers, doctors, and all other essential workers who work tirelessly to save lives. To keep everyone safe and healthy, we must follow all the rules of the government.

This episode took place on July 23rd, 2020 on New Horizon Media Arts YouTube Channel

SAFE DISTANCE SAVE LIVES

KARAN SEHMBI

Karan Sehmbi

Background

Karan Sehmbi is an established Punjabi singer who has been entertaining people for 5 years and has gained fame in the Indian music industry. Some of his popular songs that have crossed over 5 million views on YouTube include Pyar Karan, Aameen and Photo which was featured in the popular Hindi movie Luka Chuppi. COVID-19 has impacted the world in many ways and the singer shared his experience in the interview.

Episode 27

Currently, everyone is struggling to cope with the pandemic, but we're all in this together. Most industries are facing a very tough and unexpected time, but I believe that there are both positive and negative sides to every situation that teaches us something important. Today we are maintaining social distancing norms unlike before when we would go to crowded places (restaurants and malls) regularly which would cause chaos and increase the risk of spreading diseases that we are unaware of. Now we are aware of the consequences and problems we can face from going to crowded places or touching something that could potentially be infected. My recommendation/ suggestion to everyone is to take care of yourselves, your family, your loved ones, and suggest them to wear masks, sanitize themselves, and follow the advice of our experts at all times.

When it comes to my personal life, I like to keep it private and not share it with everyone in public. I have been asked multiple times by my fans about it as well. My personal life is quite small and revolves around my family members- mother, brother, and cousins. I live with some of my brothers and also speak/ video chat every day with my mother who is in *Chandigarh*. Besides, I put my mind and invest most of my time in my professional career. Having said that I'm also aware about my female fan following on social media. However, I've never really noticed that. I'm aware of all the love and support I've received from everyone, not only girls. Most people (fans) reach out to me and ask questions about the gym I go to or the diet I'm following. I want to say thank you and send lots of love to everyone who follows me and enjoys my music.

Many people have wondered and asked me whether singing was my field of interest since childhood or if I got here through luck. I wouldn't necessarily say that it's my field of interest as I was not aware of my singing talent. I was in either grade 5 or 6 and while playing games in our classroom my teacher asked me what I was talented in? He asked me to come forward and showcase my talent. There were around 40- 50 students and I didn't feel comfortable to dance so I decided to sing a song. When I began singing the first few lines, I felt different and couldn't believe that it was my voice. Everyone appreciated me that day and I realized my talent in singing. Then I competed in a few singing competitions and also became a finalist in Voice of Punjab in 2011. My professional career in singing began after PTC that brought me here.

As you all may know that the entertainment industry has been impacted severely especially in India due to the lockdown in the country. Discussion on this subject has been taking place every day amongst everyone including vocal artists, DJs, and event organizers. I have been told that they have been notified that everything is closed until October 2020. Everything depends on the number of cases that India gets and the extent to which we can manage it. Currently the music industry has completely stopped working although shooting has begun. However, we haven't been receiving the same response from people the way we did with live shows. Social media has continued to remain the strongest platform as we are all able to stay connected through these tough times.

When asked to share a message to the youth, Sehmbi said "I would like to say that we have just one life and this is the time to stay connected and happy with our loved ones. We didn't bring anything to this world nor are we going to take anything with us. Just ignore negativity, show your positive side, spread love and stay happy always".

This episode took place on July 7th, 2020 on New Horizon Media Arts YouTube Channel

SAFE DISTANCE SAVE LIVES

STEVE ELLIOT

Steve Elliot

Background

Steve Elliot is a coach, entrepreneur, speaker and overall a multi skilled and multi-faceted personality. He works with youth and professionals who are looking to improve their public speaking and communication skills. He facilitates classes that provide a safe, nurturing environment to help people develop new skills and strengthen existing ones. His mission is to help others become engaging, eloquent and exciting speakers. In this episode, he shared his experience during COVID-19 lockdown and briefly discussed the changes and adjustments he has made during these unprecedented times.

Episode 28

Despite being laid off temporarily due to COVID-19, I've remained very positive throughout. I continue to teach students during the pandemic, and am also persistent to make the required changes in my sessions in order to make it valuable and beneficial for everyone. Interpersonal engagement is an important element of communication and moving to online class has made it difficult for me to interact with students.

Something positive that came out of adapting to the new ways of teaching for me was that I was now able to take lessons with my partner in Hong Kong, which was difficult or even impossible earlier

It wasn't only self- teaching that I embraced during the pandemic, but also I interacted and tried to stay connected more with my immediate and extended family members. My children live far from me which is why I've only been able to remain in touch virtually. Whereas, some of my relatives are in long term care centres and it has been very difficult and depressing for me to live away and not be able to stay connected with them. Despite this, I've tried to continue to maintain a positive attitude and I'm thankful for the little things, which helped me work my way out of a tough phase of my life.

This episode took place on July 11th, 2020 on New Horizon Media Arts YouTube Channel

SAFE DISTANCE SAVE LIVES

HARI IYER

Hari Iyer

Background

Mr. Hari Iyer is a Professional Tax Consultant who has been running his company from home with his wife for 17 years. In this episode, he shared his experience during the lockdown, talked about how he managed to continue working and briefly discussed the ways the Canadian government has been helping taxpayers.

In addition to his professional contribution to the community, Hari is passionate about developing the youth and runs a leadership program called *Success Forever* that teaches youth skills to be successful.

Hari's philosophy of life is to have a servant mentality, as in, wanting to serve as it is only through the success of others can one be successful. He believes in the importance of being a lifelong learner as that is the only way to improve and develop oneself continuously. Today, knowledge is everywhere- in books, online websites and links, in self-development videos, and TEDx talks, and in so many other free sources. It is for us to seek the information and enrich ourselves with it. And with that learning we can help others better too. One does need to focus on self-development and leadership skills constantly to be successful in life.

Episode 30

As one would expect, the changes and uncertainties brought on by the COVID-19 pandemic in terms of lockdown and social distancing have impacted everyone in some shape or form, be it working, schooling, travelling and or even something as basic as going out for a walk. Beyond all of this, a large number of people have been impacted financially. To enable people to get through financial hardships during this difficult time, the Canadian government has implemented various schemes several of which are geared towards economic sustenance and recovery for entrepreneurs particularly small business owners.

Personally, for me I typically work 15 to 16-hour days all through the year and this has not changed. During the lockdown, I have had numerous people reaching out for advice on various aspects of the relief programs and schemes.

The Canadian government has implemented a number of programs some targeted specifically to support small businesses. There is a four-month wage subsidy offered that will cover 75% of employee wages. This has been implemented to support employee retention and enable business to continue running during this period. There is also a rent subsidy that offers a loan of 50% of the rent that does not need to be paid back to commercial landlords. In addition, students are being offered a benefit of $1250 per month to help them sustain and individuals who have lost their jobs as a result of COVID, a maximum benefit of $2000 per month.

In essence the Government has taken several steps to support Canadians in managing through this difficult time and thousands of people have taken advantage of these benefits.

This episode took place on July 14th, 2020 on New Horizon Media Arts YouTube Channel

SAFE DISTANCE SAVE LIVES

MELANIE PERIERA

Melanie Pereira

Background

Melanie Pereira is a Jack of all trades; she has many talents and has tried her hand at many things through her illustrious life. Her early adult years were spent as a NightClub Singer, she is a trained pre-primary teacher, has dabbled in sales and advertising and for the past 10 years has been an Executive Assistant at Ericsson Canada.

She is passionate about healthy living and staying fit. Her hobbies are singing and dancing.

Episode 41

I work at Ericsson which is located down the street from my house. I am very career oriented and my job is everything for me. I support over a 100 people at my company and I enjoy every minute of it. When the government announced the lockdown and advised everyone to work from home, my heart was broken. This made it difficult for me to be around my team and colleagues at work, which is what I absolutely love doing. I simply could not imagine what it would be like working without them. However, it's been a month now and I've managed to work from home well so far.

My son doesn't work from home, which is why I feel lonely a lot of the time. To overcome the frustration that resulted from loneliness at home, I started going out for walks. During lunch break from 12-1 pm, I put on my workout gear and head out for a walk, while talking to my friend or listening to some music. Another thing I do that has also helped me mentally is connecting with a friend on zoom at 3 pm to workout. We workout for about 30 mins. everyday that helps us stay fit especially during these unprecedented times.

Personally, I didn't realize how stressful this lockdown and quarantine was going to be. After 4 weeks of staying at home, I had a meltdown, as I couldn't take it anymore. One of the things I've learned during these hard times is to accept that nothing can be perfect. I've always been a perfectionist and tried to be in control at all times. I feel like we all need to learn to let go of things. It's been a struggle for me because I'm a control freak, but I've realized that life is not perfect. We need to take a deep breath and let it go or maybe take a walk in the park, enjoy nature, do some yoga, listen to some music and connect with our friends that we haven't spoken to for a while. I think we need to do all these things to enjoy and be in the moment and stay safe. One word that resonates with me the most is resilience. We should stay resilient because this too shall pass.

SAFE DISTANCE SAVE LIVES

CHERYL JAIRAJ

Cheryl Jairaj

Background

Cheryl started her career with The Co-operators back in 1997 and now 20 years later, she has achieved many milestones in her professional journey. She offers her clients Insurance products that suit their current and future needs and goals. With extensive experience in the financial services industry in both brokerages and top financial companies, she believes in providing customized solutions that suit her client's budget, lifestyle and stage of life. In addition, she has worked with some of the best people in the industry and learnt through their knowledge and expertise.

Episode 12

Starting my career back in 1997, I was awestruck with how much there was to learn about Insurance and now two decades later I realize how much I have learnt and how much more is there for me to learn. There has never been a dull moment whether it is Personal or Commercial, Life Insurance or Wealth Management. Over this period, I have acquired a deep and broad understanding of investing for the future of children in a truly unique manner. I enjoy helping my clients make sound financial decisions and have the tools and resources to help them do that. If you have questions such as: What are the best ways to save for my child? What is an alternative to a RESP? What type of Life and Health Insurance Coverage should you have, or your Auto and Home Insurance premiums have increased, how do I get better rates, then let's connect!

COVID-19 has brought about a realization for all of us to never leave anything for tomorrow, as a lot of the things we have wanted to do have been put on hold now. Most people are now making the time to stay connected with loved ones whether in person or virtually through social media. At a time when we are all confined to our homes, and many working from home, it is important to have a routine and try to create as much of an office environment as possible. In my case, I make sure I wear professional attire and get to my homework desk at 9 am every morning. I tend to follow this schedule every day to accomplish tasks while working from home.

I specialize in home insurance and a lot of my clients continue to reach out to me to gain advice on saving money. A lot of my clients don't have sufficient funds and I help them by coordinating with insurance companies and banks to waive off Non-Sufficient Funds (NSF) fees.

Maintaining a positive attitude during these unprecedented times will enable us to motivate others and keep them going. Working from home doesn't mean no work because of more flexible schedules. I think we should all get ourselves in a zone where we can tell ourselves that "we can do it". This is not much different from pre COVID times, as workwise we are doing everything we were doing before, however, we are now doing it virtually. My advice to everyone would be have a positive attitude, maintain social distancing, wear masks and don't take any of this for granted. It's better to wear a mask now than to lie in a hospital with a ventilator.

This episode took place on November 10th, 2020 on New Horizon Media Arts YouTube Channel

SAFE DISTANCE SAVE LIVES

ADITYA SETH

Aditya Seth

Background

Aditya is an award winning independent Short, Documentary & Corporate Film Maker. He is also an Academic and teaches Filmmaking (Fiction and Nonfiction) and related media studies at the Under Graduate and Postgraduate levels. He is an Educational Consultant for the Newport Film School University of South Wales, UK. He wishes to create a culture & environment for Independent Short" Documentary Filmmaking in the country sans prejudice or censorship, which is self-sustaining. He has his own Film and media institute The Indian Academy of Shorts in Delhi to actualize this goal. Currently the President of The Indian Documentary Producers Association.

Episode 24

I am a filmmaker and have been in this industry for more than 30 years. I started off in Delhi and then moved to Bombay where I've been living for 25 years now. I have primarily been making documentaries and TV shows. I also run a small academy, where I teach filmmaking in Delhi. Other than filmmaking, I offer consultancy services for educational institutions and am a part of the Indore Career Film Association.

Since the lockdown took effect in India, the two things I miss most are my morning newspaper and my evening walk time. I used to walk 5 km a day and that helped me stay active. However, that has stopped now. As far as my professional life goes, I was in the process of completing a course which has suddenly stopped. Also, I did not get to see the final plots of the film we had planned because shooting had to be cancelled as soon as the lockdown was announced.

Personally, the lockdown hasn't affected me too much because I've always worked from home. Given the pause to many elements of film making, I have felt the need to express myself creatively in some other way during this period. This has taken shape in the form of writing poetry and sharing via social media. Everyday I get some casual thought which then turns into a poem of 3-4 lines that I post on to my social media pages. I believe that my recent poems resonated with a lot of people of my age, as it was my response/ reaction to events that have occurred since the outbreak of COVID-19.

In referring to people my age, I mean people who like in the city, are secure and are able to afford and survive this lockdown. Unlike the western world, most people in India tend not to follow rules and instructions imposed by the government and they always get away with it. There is a lot of disbelief and mistrust amongst the people here. Overall, we are not disciplined and just not willing to conform to what we are asked to do. Also, we tend to be very religious and superstitious, which makes it difficult for us to believe that there could be a virus that could potentially harm or kill us. We think by praying to God or doing things the old-fashioned way like resorting to herbal teas we can save ourselves from getting infected. This is why we Indians have an attitude and belief that "nothing can happen to us".

This episode took place on June 30th, 2020 on New Horizon Media Arts YouTube Channel

SAFE DISTANCE SAVE LIVES

RANJAN BAKSHI

Ranjan Bakshi

Background

Ranjan comes from a strong software background and was leading the technology department in the SAP practice at KPMG Sydney for more than 5 years. With an MBA degree from Griffith University, he founded his own company in 2002. Prospecta was his baby and for the last 18 years he has played various roles within Prospecta. Always passionate about designing solutions that address the core concern of business operation and governance. His focus has been to have solutions that form the foundation of any business improvement or compliance related initiative. He is also an avid trekker and fitness

Episode 13

When it comes to accomplishing tasks, virtually, I think advanced and modern technologies have made it possible for us to excel at it at this point of time. In fact, I named the product I launched Master Data Online 12 years ago, where the data online is mastering our lives today. I believe that we are all fortunate to be able to continue to accomplish even from home. For my company, working from home is not a new concept as a lot of our team members have been working and dealing with the customers remotely. Since the lockdown, the whole process of working remotely has become more structured than before and our customers now expect to be served virtually instead of in-person.

Even though many people are working from home well, a lot of people can't work from home because their jobs involve only practical skills. Also, not everyone has adequate space, facilities and internet connection to be able to work remotely. I believe that 99% of people and industries have been impacted both directly and indirectly due to the lockdown. Despite this, people and companies are making changes and finding creative solutions to accomplish work virtually. For instance my gym trainer continues to give me sessions over zoom and even though it's done virtually I sweat the same way and am still able to stay fit.

I actually travelled to New York in March and after returning back to Australia I had to quarantine for 14 days. After completing the quarantine, I was allowed to go out so then I took the time to explore nature and go for walks around the parks here. Also, since the outbreak I've been spending a lot of quality time with my wife and kids. Since I travel a lot I miss my family and this lockdown has actually helped us care about little things in life like spending time with family. Within a month I travelled across 3 countries including India, US, and Australia for work purposes. I would like to say that out of all 3 the US is not tackling this pandemic crisis well.

New York City is very densely populated, and it is also a major travel destination which is why the situation there has worsened since the outbreak of COVID-19. I believe that the situation in places like the US and Spain could have been handled better, but at the same time people don't realize the importance of staying at home while the death tolls continue to rise. I remember when I was in Seattle people didn't even bother to follow the rules and they kept saying that it will never reach New York. Within 2 weeks the virus had only reached New York but people were suffering and dying there.

Also, I think that Australia has handled the situation very well, and the prime minister has proven to be an excellent leader. The same India also tackled this crisis well by announcing a 24/7 lockdown for the whole country and increasing the number of tests. I think people should learn a lesson now and follow the rules because there may be another pandemic that might hit us in the future. I think countries should invest more in their health care system than in weapons of warfare. We need to prepare ourselves, because there could be another virus in the future that could be more dangerous.

My message to everyone is to believe that everything will be okay and just hang in there. I know it can get very frustrating and you may be tempted to go out, but just remember that you will hurt others if you break the rules of the lockdown. Be patient and remember that this too shall pass.

This episode took place on May 30th, 2020 on New Horizon Media Arts YouTube Channel

SAFE DISTANCE SAVE LIVES

SEAN C DWYER

Sean D Actor

Background

Sean is a theatre artist, actor, producer, maker of short films. For a decade he was associated with theater. He has studied film as art, as artefact and as production, he has made countless short films, he has participated in ever bigger productions including the Terminator 2:3-D show at Universal Studios Japan. It has been a journey! In and among that journey is a lot of international volunteering, a theatre youth group in India, a summer festival with orphans in Japan, films with kids in Ecuador, cinema therapy workshops in Montreal and a Restorative Justice program in Los Angeles. Alongside creation within the film world, his life has always and will always have an aspect of participation within the world of social justice.

Episode 25

My experience in the entertainment industry has been very interesting. In fact, last year I was performing at Universal Studios in Japan until my contract ended on March 21st, 2020. I had planned on flying back to Los Angeles on March 23rd to do some work related to acting, meet my dad and some old friends, do some hiking and make my way to Toronto in early May. Universal Studios were closed in early March and for the last 3 weeks in Japan I was not in lockdown because it took place late here. I got back to Canada and it's been over 2 months since I'm in lockdown. I stayed aware of the situation in LA and then had to make changes to my plan to end up in Canada. I'm lucky to have travelled a bit and have made friends from various parts of the World including India, Africa, Europe and North America. It's been very fascinating to connect with people from all over the world and see the kind of experiences that we are sharing as humans. I think that this pandemic is making us realize the humanity in us and that we are all in this together.

When it comes to my career, I've actually been in the acting profession since I was 11 years old. My dad watched the biography of Michael Caine one night on A&E which inspired us to get into action. So, we called the local community theatre and somehow that same evening at around 10 pm within 45 minutes Ann Curio Bryan came by the house to give us the information. Somehow, I managed to skip over the 45 person waiting list to get into the youth group. Also, before that I made films with friends anytime we had a video camera and then I did a variety of schooling too. Since 2007 I have been making short films of all kinds even while I studied law and became a lawyer. After completing my education in law school and finishing internship, I was in California for 2 years in a legal capacity. In 2017 I decided to give myself a year to become a

professional actor which continued from 2018, 2019 and brought me here in 2020. I just wanted to see the response and feedback of the audience after trying out acting in Japan and Canada. I've been reached by a lot of people for film opportunities which involve commercial productions too. Since the outbreak of COVID-19, I've been receiving the Canadian Emergency Response Benefit (CERB) from the Canadian government. However, I will not take the maximum amount offered by the government, because there are opportunities that I believe I can create within this environment, not necessarily well paid though. For example- even when I was in Japan, I had started to do audiobooks on ACX Amazon Audible which was more of a fun opportunity that didn't pay much. However, there is a possibility for me to create a home studio and then just go through a bunch of books.

In a normal routine, if I spend a day or so in my apartment, I become very frustrated. However, since we are all in this together, I think we can all benefit by connecting virtually. Staying in touch with people virtually means that one is not alone at home because that is much worse. It's all about keeping yourself busy and doing a variety of things. There are a lot of rumors about conspiracy, but I would recommend to not believe everything that we are being told. It's good to put on your work clothes, or touch base with friends, or even have virtual dates.

This episode took place on July 4th, 2020 on New Horizon Media Arts YouTube Channel

SAFE DISTANCE SAVE LIVES

ASIS SETHI

Asis Sethi

Background

Asis Sethi has always been in the entertainment industry - smiling and making others smile. Her career boasts of success both off-screen and on-screen, as she mixes and mingles with directing, writing, producing, acting and hosting. Asis started a film company in 2019 called Fly Away Films Inc which focuses on making films that start a conversation. Films recently directed and produced by her include **A Bloody Mess and Still**.

Her most recent work includes producing and directing a three-episode television show for Scotiabank and OMNI TV titled **Welcome To Canada** which highlighted real life stories told by immigrants of Canada. Asis is also the Art Director for Bollywood Film Fame Canada, a quarterly Bollywood magazine published in Toronto covering exclusive interviews of celebrities from Bollywood - be it within the music industry, acting industry, or those making an impact within the South Asian community and beyond. As part of her television reporting and involvement in Bollywood Film Fame Canada, Asis has interviewed celebrities and covered the red carpet at the Toronto International Film Festival for several years.

With her ear to the ground and her eyes to the sky, Asis has a multi-faceted approach to all things film and entertainment and a keen sense of awareness of what the public desires, as a result of her broad work experience.

Episode 32

My experience amidst the COVID-19 crisis has been both challenging and positive this far. While challenged to keep my two young children engaged and positively occupied with the schools closed, it's also been great as I've been able to spend a lot of time with them. I've been able to squeeze in a lot of activities including bhangra, hip-hop and Bollywood dancing. Along with this, I have also managed to carve out time to work on my films and television productions.

A positive impact of working from home has been the elimination of my long and often tiring commute from Brampton to downtown Toronto where I work. This has also enabled me to spend a lot of quality time with my husband and kids. To make the best use of the new normal state, I have created a schedule whereby I wake up early in the morning, get the kids showered, dressed, fed and ready for the day before getting on with my daily work schedule. After attending to work priorities for a couple of hours, I take care of household chores whilst making sure the kids are gainfully engaged in activities like reading, writing, playing versus watching hours of TV.

I believe that it is very important to educate the kids about COVID-19. My 3-year-old may not understand what I'm trying to tell her, but she does know the word "coronavirus". So, when I tell her that they cannot do certain activities like going to the beach, she knows that's because of COVID-19. In contrast, my 6-year-old knows exactly what the virus and its consequences are and the importance of sanitizing. In my opinion it's important to educate the kids about the virus so they develop good hygiene habits that will stand them in good stead.

On the career front, I'm honored to be a part of Women in Film and Television (WIFT). They have been very supportive of my work as well as the work of other diverse women who have contributed to the film and television industry in Canada. They have acknowledged my film **A Bloody Mess** and some of my other work for which I'm grateful. I would like to thank my sister Armin, and other close friends Daisy, Amreeen and Shweata who supported me in the making of **A Bloody Mess**. I fondly remember attending the Toronto International Film Festival with them in 2018 to promote this film. This was a very memorable moment as in the past, we always attended the Film Festival to interview celebrities standing on the other side of the barricades, dreaming of being on the other side one day!

There are a lot of female issues that need to be covered especially in the South Asian community. This is where the idea for our film emerged and is based on menstruation and the taboos that surround it in the South Asian community. It started with Armin and I kicking off the writing process after which Think Brown Media got involved and helped us with the project. After the film was written, we began casting where a lot of pre-production work was required. The making of the film took a year and a lot of work had to be done to prepare and get ready for the shooting. The post-production work was also quite consuming as we needed to make sure everything was done perfectly. The sound engineering on the film was done by Steven Edgeback, a Canadian Screens Awards winner. Daniel the DOP of the film too is a very talented individual who contributed a lot to this project. Overall, the film was a team effort and each member contributed to the successful completion of the film.

A Bloody Mess was first screened and premiered on June 7th at the Houston Asian American Pacific Islander Film Festival. Since the outbreak of COVID-19, all the film festivals are taking place virtually and our film will be screening at other festivals including- AFIN International Film Festival, LA Edge Film Awards, and the Toronto Female Film Festival. At the Houston International Film Festival, we won the Remy award, which is considered to be the biggest honor for a short filmmaker. This film festival is known to have kick-started the careers of several famous Hollywood filmmakers such as George Lucas and Steven Spielberg. In addition, this film has won other awards including Florence and Queen Palm in California.

Armin and I wrote the script of the film together as we felt that this was a very important topic that needed to be surfaced and discussed. I believe that this film served as a voice for a lot of South Asian women and women in general. **A Bloody Mess** brings to light issues in our community related to menstruation which are important to me as a filmmaker and as a woman. In South Asian communities, women face issues normalizing conversations surrounding menstruation or even having discussions about it with their male family members. Personally, I've dealt with such problems myself, and in the past instead of saying I'm on my periods I would say I'm not feeling well. I believe that women should be able to freely share how they are feeling and comfortably say that "I'm on my period". These are some of the issues this film explores and the purpose of it is to help women start a conversation comfortably about menstruation.

For the future, I have a few films in the pipeline which includes a short film named Still that is almost complete and will be screened at film festivals soon. My other short film is a monologue on postpartum depression that we are waiting to shoot. My sister and I are in the process of writing a feature film about a disempowered South Asian housewife who wants to put her shoes back on, go back to the basketball courts and start fulfilling her basketball dream to show her daughter that she is more than just a housewife and a mother. By this she desires to empower herself and prove that she is an individual first.

I'm a firm believer of equality between men and women and have seen gender inequality for a very long time. When I had my first daughter, I thought to myself that I don't want her to have a future like most South Asian women where they are judged because they are females. I don't want my daughters to think that it's acceptable for boys to do anything and get away with it and as girls they should not be doing that. I'm passionate about raising awareness about issues that women face through films so that we can have a better society and future for our daughters.

This episode took place on August 8th, 2020 on New Horizon Media Arts YouTube Channel

SAFE DISTANCE SAVE LIVES

DEAN BOWY

Dean Boye

Background

He is currently a social worker, who was also a Financial advisor for three years with Blue cross Jamaica, and is currently a MDRT qualifier. Before moving to Canada, he was a conventions Manager for 5 years at Palace Resorts. Currently, he works at Cawthra Road Shelter and works through a program to get homeless men and women office treats and an accommodation.

We get each person that reaches out for help housing in the region of Peel. There are many kinds of people who reach out to us for help, such as people who get involved in drugs and end up becoming homeless, people who land into financial trouble due to unemployment and can no longer afford to pay their mortgages. This includes both Canadian residents and foreigners.

I got involved in this type of social work after having volunteered in a homeless shelter in Jamaica. The issues related to homelessness have gotten worse as a result of the COVID-19 pandemic, due to cuts in provincial funding. This led to many problems for people who used to get housing in 6 months with the help of this government funding. We find that refugees reach out to us for help and make their way here which creates a shortage of space and resources for women who are victims of domestic violence. Over the years, with more refugees immigrating to Canada, there has been lack of space for other segments of the population, as the number of refugees reaching out has substantially increased. A segment of society that I believe suffer from homelessness the most are men.

During the winters, problems related to homelessness worsen, as people can't tolerate the cold and become in desperate need of basic necessities like food and accommodation. In our shelter, we make compromises when the number of people that show up exceed our limit, in order to ensure that we have 4 spots left for women at all times. For this, we are compelled to refuse to help men to save space for women. People reach out to us everyday for help, and we provide housing for 2 weeks until they receive funding from Ontario Works. Also, oftentimes people who have mental illnesses reach out to us for help and ensure that they are taken care of in a Wellness Centre or other appropriate places. We try to help people with mental illness, which is why they end up staying for more than 2 weeks.

The only form of donations we accept are fresh food and new clothes. We ensure that people in our shelter are treated respectfully, and they never feel abandoned, which is why we ask everyone to only donate fresh food and new clothes.

Personally, my life has been significantly affected as a result of COVID-19. I wasn't able to graduate from my college because I had to leave Canada to take care of a family member who fell severely sick. Also, I work at a retirement home, and I've been working with vulnerable people since the beginning of COVID-19. Due to the risk of spreading the virus, I lost my accommodation in Brampton. I was able to get a place in Oshawa, but it has been a struggle for me, as I have to commute back and forth to Mississauga.

My message to everyone is to not ignore the rules and restrictions of the lockdown. It is our responsibility to keep not only ourselves but others safe too. You must know that this virus is killing everyone and it's not a conspiracy.

SAFE DISTANCE SAVE LIVES

JAY WIJESUNDARA

Jay Wijesundara

Background

Jay (Jayarani) Wijesundara is an Author, Daily blogger for (Amazing Quotes), international personnel and professional coach to Toastmaster and Women in Retail. She specializes in uncovering the power of soul using "Practicing the Pause" to help a person achieve fulfillment and heart-centered success. She has launched her book "Reengineer Yourself". She was born and raised in Colombo, Sri Lanka and moved to Canada in 1994 to attend the University of Waterloo. Her aim is to make a difference by helping, assisting and guiding young girls who immigrate to Canada and struggle to adjust in a new country.

Episode 31

Amidst the COVID-19 pandemic, I took the time to write my book and finish my daily blogs too. I tend to write at least 3 times in a week. Also, I've been continuing work as a manager at Starbucks. There are two reasons Starbucks is open during the pandemic, which include to allow access to the public and most importantly provide coffee and snacks for free to the frontline workers.

Personally, myself and my family's lives haven't been significantly impacted, as my husband and sons continue to work during the lockdown. The only change in our lives that occurred as a result of COVID-19 is that we have been cooking more than usual and trying out new recipes regularly. I've always managed time well with work, writing, and family. I believe that at the end of the day, it's all about prioritizing commitments to ultimately achieve a work-life balance. I try to contribute to our society in some ways, like offering to pay for frontline workers who come to Starbucks and also offering treats to young people who reach out to me for help. As a family, we collect and send clothes, shoes, and school supplies to charities and orphanages in third war countries like Sri Lanka. Receiving gifts from overseas gives joy to the children there which makes me very happy.

My upcoming book "Reengineer Yourself" will be sold in 7 countries including Canada, India, Denmark, Australia, Italy, US, and UK. I would like to mention that in this book I have added 5 ideas for simple acts of kindness which include- buy a coffee for someone, compliment someone, offer help to someone, start a conversation with someone sitting nearby, and try to speak positively about everyone you know. Every 1 cent of $1 my book makes will go towards helping the children in Sri Lanka. My motive behind writing this book is not only to monetize but to motivate and inspire people, and help the children in third war countries.

This episode took place on July 25th, 2020 on New Horizon Media Arts YouTube Channel

Episode 34 - Power Within - Inspiring stories of women entrepreneurs

Panel discussion

Dwania Peele - thank you for doing this amazing job. C19 ruined some of our plans, we had this grand plan of bringing 5 amazing women together to share their stories of becoming entrepreneurs and our 1st book. We had everything planned to use March, the International women's month to promote the book via a series of events, including a book signing. Then COVID happened. The name of the book is Power Within. We were going to share our powerful stories of 5 women, representing 5 countries, Mexico, India, Guyana, USA and the UK. The book was a passion project of ours. We never thought being an author was something we were going to do. Being an immigrant woman coming to Canada and becoming an entrepreneur, it was important that they share their stories. We launched the book in February and had a slew of events that we were planning to attend in March and April and then that whole state of emergency happened and we had to stop. We were all looking forward to it and the lockdown stole that from us.

Genoveva Vazquez - The book was an experience that was meant to be for me. I did not know Dwania. A friend of mine was organizing a conference that I signed up to attend and this is when I came to know about the book. I met Dwania at the conference two weeks later and told her that I wanted to participate but the deadline was very close and would not work for me. She then turned around and said that the deadline was going to move. I then joined her community at the right time, met the deadline and the book happened. Thereafter, I went away for a wedding to Mexico knowing that the events were happening and that I would miss some but be able to attend others and then the day after I returned from Mexico, the lockdown happened.

Rituu Nebb - Dwania and I go back more than 6 years. We met through a common friend and meet every few months for a meal and we always support each other in our journeys. What she has showcased in her book is the camaraderie, how women actually bring the support system together. When she mentioned the book, I wanted to understand what it was all about. As I heard about it, I realized that Mallika was working on something similar. I realized that both initiatives would complement one another. I was apprehensive about the book. However, Dwania convinced me that I had nothing to worry about as they had an editor. I want to thank my sister who helped me with everything. I am not a big book worm. It was daunting for me but I completed it. I find it hard to believe that I wrote and I am an author. It's a big achievement for me. That's an excitement that you hear in my voice. Thanks to Dwania for that.

Dwania Peele - I never thought I would be an author. However, when it was presented to me 7 years ago when we were in business and I never thought I would do it as I can barely write an email. I was inspired by people like you all because I felt that needed to be some way to share your stories.

I wanted this book to be about everyone else because of my immigrant women small business expos. I would have so many people come up to me at these expos and say, Dwania, we are so happy that you are an immigrant woman organizing these expos. We are so happy that we have this comfortable space and also, people don't look at us as though we want to start businesses.

As I heard this I felt sad as the narrative is always, Immigrants - labor force and not Immigrants - entrepreneurs. I wanted people to see that we are more than just the labor force and I wanted other immigrants to read the stories of these wonderful women and feel inspired to continue on their entrepreneurial journey. This was early last year that I decided that we should do a collaborative book. I did a lot of research and realized that people are charging thousands of dollars to do collaborative books. I realized that it does not cost so much to publish a book. I have a dear friend Matthew Ink, who did the entire cover both front and back for free. The bulk of the fee came in for paying the editors. To have that support and to be able to give that support to others is what I really wanted to do. So when I put out that call for this project I wanted to make sure that I had women from unique backgrounds represented as representation matters. I wanted other women to see themselves in these stories. There was a point when I could have stopped all this. At the point when I started to get all the submissions, I had just had a lumpectomy. I was just starting Chemotherapy. This book happened while I was going through Chemo. This was my only project and I said I am going to fight through this to make it happen. I still have the promo copy and will never let go of it as it means so much to me. It's not about me. I did not say that I am the author. I said that I had compiled it. It's about everyone sharing their story. Just listening to the stories at the expo is heart wrenching. I cannot say that I have been through very tough times. A lot of people in these stories have been through very tough times and they have come out of it at the top. They found that power deep within in order to succeed.

Dwania Peele - I am the executive director and founder of the Canadian Small Business Women. It took birth from the fact that I felt that there was a need for people who did not grow up in an entrepreneurial household to get information on how to start a business. We aim to be a collaborative group where we can connect people with all the tools that they need in order to propel a small business.

When we put out the call for the book, we got a lot of emails. People were interested and first and foremost for me was that I responded to people from different backgrounds. That part was very deliberate. I wanted to make sure that they understood that the point of this book was to inspire others with their stories. They could include as much or as little as they wanted to but had to make sure that the reader felt inspired. I got a lot of questions on how they should write their stories. The "how" was up to them. We have Natasha who told her story in a flashback present moment format. She would tell a story of her childhood and then talk about the present moment and then back to her childhood. Doujone McLarty, who is my younger sister, from the US went through a lot as a single parent and still goes through it. She wanted to make sure that her connection was for the single parent entrepreneur. She wants them to know that she still went to school and went through everything she needed to and is still coming up on top. We had Christine Rae who had a unique story. Her journey was easier relative to some others, but I wanted to have a story that was not all about the struggle but more so about striving for excellence and making it to the top. I wanted to make sure there was balance in the book.

Genoveva Vazquez - I was an accountant, a CPA. When I went through getting my designation, I went through Life Coaching and ended up as an entrepreneur becoming a Coach. I had no writing experience and it was not my calling. I had no writing experience. However as a coach you need to be able to share your stories. Also as a coach I have worked on myself right left and center. I was therefore able to share my story in a more reflective way rather than making it all about the struggle. At that time I had a guy who was helping me with marketing and I asked him if he could help me write a biography and he said he could for sure and he started writing it in third person style. To me, I had no idea how to start and he helped, however he was not able to deliver on time. I then had to take over. He gave me a general framework and I continued with it. At the end I had to write it. As much as you share with someone who can write for you, they have not lived it. I did not know how to write, but I had lived it and wrote it the way I had lived it. Then Dwania asked me to change it to first person instead of third person to make it more personal. I then changed. Since then I have become more familiar with writing and have been writing blogs. It is something I am enjoying now, however if you had asked me 5 years ago, I would have denied it.

Rituu Nebb - It is all about what you want to do. Every person has multiple things to do. Life is all about prioritizing. When I have a deadline, I prioritize. I am a multitasker. I cannot focus on one thing at a time. That's just me. It becomes boring and slow. My husband knows that and even calls me ADHD. I need to have at least three things I am doing at the same time and this is something I have learnt about myself. I realize that sometimes when you do not focus on one thing at a time, you cannot give anything hundred percent. When the book came along, I had to prioritize although I was busy with dancing. Luckily I have a lot of time as I don't have kids. I run a dance school, paint, am part of toastmasters, do house chores. Everyone can do it, they just need to prioritize. I worked on it at night time when I was able to focus. I had to switch off the music to work on this as music is usually a part of everything I do. As you go back and think about your struggles you break down. I had to work on it at night over a month as I could not work on it continuously.

Favourite sentences from the book

Rituu Nebb - Everyone has challenges in life. The only way to go ahead is letting go of the past.

Genoveva Vazquez - We need to read those stories to remember that we will go through things, however at the end things will work out.

Dwania Peele - I am very thankful to the ladies for sharing their stories as this is not easy to do. This is very brave and will inspire others.

This episode took place on September 5th, 2020 on New Horizon Media Arts YouTube Channel

SAFE DISTANCE SAVE LIVES

UJJWAL ROY CHOWDHURY

Ujjwal Roy Chowdhuri alias Ricky

Background

Ujjwal Roy Chowdhuri is a Bollywood composer and music director and producer. He has worked on different projects such as movies, TV serials, albums and also composed background scores. Ujjwal's singing talent has been complimented and praised by several famous singers such as Asha Bhonsle and Shaan.

Nirupama was a finalist in the Sa Re Ga Ma Pa television program in India aired on Zee TV. It was after this win that she joined the music industry.

Episode 26

Ujjwal - In different ways we are experiencing different things now. We used to go for recordings, meetings etc before the lockdown. However that is not possible now. I used to compose tracks and make music in my studio even before the lockdown. That has not changed. We used to meet friends before the lockdown which we are not able to do now. A song for my friends - Yaron, dosti, badi hi haseen hai……..

Nirupama - There is very little happening now. All recording is happening at home. I record it on my cell phone and share via Whatsapp.

Ujjwal - I have a music programming set up. I compose there. It has various software to produce music and has so many tracks, chords etc. We do the mixing in this system and send the composition to the singers. The singers use two phones - one to play the track and the other to record the song. There is no leakage. The singer then sends me the recording and I do the mixing and then complete the song. Before the lockdown we used to record the voices in big recording studios in Mumbai but now that is not possible.

Music is still produced traditionally in the western world with symphonies and orchestras. In India that is not possible now. I produce the music in the production system using the voice track

Nirupama - COVID times with the lockdown is difficult for everyone, but especially so for the newcomers/strugglers. We have to stay strong and hold on to the hope that everything will get better. I am holding on to this mindset.

Ujjwal - Before the lockdown, I was able to travel often to see my family and friends in Bengal but am not able to do that now. I am so grateful for social media and the internet connectivity via which I talk to my mother, brothers and childhood friends. I miss all of them. I miss playing football with my friends and the traditional food in bengal. I love my mother so much. I will sing a song for her.

Music Video about Corona - Some people are scared and are suffering so much because of Corona. They are also worried about the future. I created this video to encourage people. I spoke to my friend who works for T-Series (music company) and he said that it was a good idea and that's how the video was born.

This episode took place on July 4th, 2020 on New Horizon Media Arts YouTube Channel

Episode -18 The Protest 2020

Background

Black lives matter protests began during the pandemic after the death of a 46-year-old black man George Floyd. The protests in support of this movement caused a lot of rage amongst all Americans which eventually led to a global outcry for justice. Floyd's death took place in police custody and it raised important issues related to racism, white supremacy and police brutality in the US.

Anti-black racism rally in Mississauga - Black Lives Matter

Unrest is everywhere and it is the marginalized people that are facing it.

Panel discussion with eminent community leaders - Kyle Mitchell, Stachen Frederick, Shelley Jarrett, Kareem

Panelist background

Kyle Mitchell - He is Toastmasters member and a criminal justice reform advocate. He has supported the innocence project over the years and has also supported the women's prisons in Austin, Texas - Truth be told, not for profit. Now he is involved with all the protests here in the US with the Black Lives Matter movement. It is close to home to him as he is in an inter-racial marriage with a black woman.

Stachen Frederick - Stachen runs an organization which supports the black community- Braid for Aids. This organization promotes HIV AIDS awareness and provides the black community access to resources. She has worked in the prison with young men and helped them not just navigate through the criminal justice system but also around sexual health, mental health. As the executive of a Charity that supports the black youth, she is providing them with a variety of services which include- academic, employment and community development. Also, she currently teached grant writing and community development at a college in Toronto.

Shelley Jarrett -Shelley is an Entrepreneur, Magazine Publisher, Speaker, Mentor, and Documentary Film Producer. She publishes a lifestyle magazine which is called SMJ magazine and is about arts and entertainment, beauty and fashion, health and wellness, faith and community. She also provides a platform to businesses in the community to allow them to tell their business story. She recently produced a woman's documentary *W'AT ABOWT US*, which was an award-winning documentary, about eight women from all five major cultural backgrounds who tell their stories of abuse in diverse locations. She is also a group facilitator at the Canadian Centre for Women Empowerment which is an organization that helps women who are victims of domestic violence to enable them to tell their stories.

Kareem (Shelley's son) - He is a community leader and activist especially for at risk youth. I live in the Jane and Finch community in the west end of Toronto. In the front lines I see things that the youth are affected by and the way all these things are going on. I am one of them and know what they go through. As a leader I try to use my voice to help the voiceless as the truth either gets washed away or is unheard. He is also a writer and is currently developing a documentary with his mother which is called **When they don't come home**. This documentary shows how women who are mothers experience trauma when their sons don't come home. This is a debilitating fear felt by a lot of mothers who raise sons.

Panel Discussion

Kareem - What has happened during COVID-19 is that people have been able to center themselves. People now understand what is like to be out of a job, they understand what it means to be out of food. Before this many people did not have an understanding of the reality that racialized black bodies, those that live in poverty experience. But now, I think there is that understanding. Furthermore, I think there is sensitization of everything that is happening and here in Toronto, we have not been immune from police brutality. I speak of my experience when I was a counselor in my career where I was held at gunpoint by the police here in Toronto while I was helping a young man. So even as we do the work out in the community, many of us are putting ourselves at risk. We are now sharing our stories and understanding that this cannot go on and that black lives matter. We were trying to do peaceful protests for a long time so Kapernick knew, we took long walks and nothing happened. I am not one to take a black kid and walk. I do my protest in a different way within the four walls of the organization I work with which is ensuring that there is funding for the development of our young black boys. That is my protest and my element of bringing change. Some work in policy and in government to try and make change and some freedom to take cardboard and walk down the street. I think we are all just fed up with the policing of our bodies in so many different ways and this is not just a police issue, this is other white people policing our bodies from our employment standpoint from where you know there is micro management and there is micro aggression. It's a feeling when you walk into the store and someone decides to follow you and it's the boiling up of all of this that has resulted in this sort of protest that we are seeing.

I have seen different kinds of policing, over policing and underpolicing because where I moved to in Toronto was considered a very risky area. The Jane and Finch area is considered dangerous but I have more positive experiences with police here than in Peel growing up. So seeing that difference, it gave me an understanding and a balance of seeing the issue with how police react to young black males especially. It's more of a worldwide issue. I have friends in America, in different states, a friend of mine is in Michigan and another friend in Pennsylvania and they are saying the same thing that you are saying here as well Kyle. I am seeing more openings for structural change and that's the one thing that we have been lacking for the longest time. We've been dealing with the same issues of police brutality and even being caught on the camera, the Rodney King issue was 30 years ago and the same thing is going on even today. There is a big opportunity for structural change and that is a positive way to look at it. As a young boy in the high risk area, I too get disheartened sometimes and feel that nothing is going to change but now I feel that there is some hope given this global outcry for justice. This is a little bit different from other times as people from all countries and nationalities are standing up against this and this is the first time in my lifetime that I am seeing it happen.

Shelley Jarrett - This week has been very hard for lots of black mothers and grandmothers and I can identify with all of them as I have been a paranoid mother. I used to call my son all the time as I was anxious and this would drive him crazy and he would say, "mom get a life". However, I know the anxiety even before all this happened. It's a good thing now that there are cameras and social media so people really know what is going on and what these black men have to go through. Also all these stories are highlighting police brutality and if someone was not filming it we would not know. There is heightened awareness. I am happy to hear the Prime Minister say that there is institutional racism and that we are going to do something about it. We actually want to see change now and I am optimistic that there will be change with all this media coverage and stories coming out.

Why does the conviction take so much time even though there is evidence? Is there a need for change to the justice system?

Kyle - There is a need for change in the justice system in the United States and in many countries. The system can do so much better as there is a lot of power in the hands of the prosecutors. In this case we were so blessed and lucky that Minnesota had prosecutors that were on the right side of the history on this case. They aggressively and at the instruction and encouragement of the governor and mayor did the right thing. In so many places in the US and other countries the prosecutors overcharge and use the law as a weapon against black men. What we saw here was a quicker than usual response of charging and arresting cops. I am proud of them. Almost a year ago to the day of George Floyd's murder, I was searving on a jury of a child abuse case and I got to see how important it is to get it right the first time. We took three or four days longer than they thought it was going to and that was worth it because the person we ended up convicting deserved it and if we had made a mistake and rushed it it could have been horrific for the victim and for the legacy that some of these cases, even small ones make on society.

Stachen - What I think has happened is a quick response to people's protests, as there was a careful articulation of charges. Previously people have looked at this as an individualized issue. However we know that in society there is the microsystem, the meso system etc and we therefore have to look at the broader structure that is impacting our communities. We need to think about the system that finds it acceptable to shoot a black man or step on the kneel of a black man and kill him slowly. In Toronto a young woman died from falling 25 feet from her apartment building and now people are saying different things like, she had mental health issues, her mother was on drugs, which are all rhetorics. Do all these things that people want to talk about matter as she falls to her death? What people are now understanding is the structural racism and how many white girls, that the police have been called to support and who didn't die from police brutality. How is it that a black girl fell 25 floors and died? Our community needs justice. We are somewhat behind the United States in terms of seeing swift justice even though we have black men who are the police heads of some of our major cities. I am sorry to say that they are our token black men who are there doing good work, but we are not seeing the changes we want to see in terms of swift action when it comes to police brutality. We still see cases of officers on leave with pay whereas in the United States we saw swift action in them getting fired right away. I think we here in Canada have a long way to move forward to structural racism.

Kareem - In terms of structural change, it all comes down to changing the mindset. They should not even be questioning why this black man lost his life. Regardless of what type of person he is, or is not, you should feel bad about a person losing their life. What is holding some black men down is the negative imagery of them. Regardless of what they hear at home, it's very hard to overcome the impact of this external negative imagery. It takes a very strong will of self and knowledge of self to overcome that. One thing that will help is creating positive reinforcements, images of black men on TV as doctors, lawyers and professionals in all kinds of fields and not just a stereotypical basketball player, entertainer, although they can be great at those professions, people want to see them in white collar jobs. This is education for everybody, not just black people. Everyone would love to hear about the great things that black people have done, not just the slavery stories that are horrific to listen to. .

Shelley Jarrett - I can identify with a lot of black moms as this is not new, this is something that has been happening from the time they were in school and it starts very young. It starts in elementary with the black kids being accused of doing this and that, probably even starts at the daycare or the even earlier in the playground. As a mother I was constantly anxious. It doesn't matter how much we teach them to be respectful if they are stopped by the police. It does not give a guarantee that they will not be killed or hurt. My husband is Caucasian, white Canadian and we have been stopped only once in eleven years and it was a traffic violation. I know this would be different if I was with my son and don't know how many times I would have been stopped. There is a difference.

Kareem - If my mother hears any news of a black man getting hurt in the west end, she reaches out to me right away to find out if I am okay. I can completely understand the debilitating fear that black mothers must live under all the time. No mother should live under the fear of her child not coming home.

Stachen - Statistics show that blackmen are stopped more than any other race and gender and then people talk about what is happening in the justice system and how many are convicted for the same crime and we see so many people locked up in prison for drug charges having 20 year sentences and then someone who is not black will get two years off this and then two years off that. This is discrimination.

Kyle - Reggie Watts, the DJ on James Corden's late night show, he's biracial and he says that he has been trying his whole life to not be black, he is just trying to be a human.

Stachen - I don't think Trump is not taking any action. I think he is taking action. It's just that it's in a negative light and I think that is part of the reason for the fueling of the tensions and the riots that we are seeing. For his entire tenure we've seen a divide in many different things whether it is a race divide or a gender divide. The things that he says breeds the heat. As we look here in Canada the Premier three days ago made a statement that structural racism does not exist in Canada. While we may have our issues, it is not the same as in the United States. You have different types of racism, you have covert and you have overt. In the States, they will just call you the n-word and this way at least you know upfront what you are dealing with. Here in Canada it is unfortunate because we are so polite and people are not seeing that type of racism but it does exist. A couple of days later the Premier retracted his statement and said that structural racism does exist and that there is a need to talk about it and have resources for the Ontario black youth action. The Ontario black youth action plan was something that was created under the previous party and as soon as they came into power that program was relaunched.

Then all of a sudden in the last three days there has been a mobilization of resources, where they say this is what we are going to do in the community. Again unfortunately do we know if this is authentic? Do they understand that the UN has proclaimed this decade as the decade of people of African descent and that there is a mandate by the UN where certain sorts of reforms need to take place in the community for black people. This is a bigger thing than coming out and reporting and saying that we are giving this money for reform. It is more than the money. In the system, we see so many different organizations generously donating right now. However, as we look at who are at the C-suite in these organizations, we see white people and they just don't get it. Unless there is representation and understanding in all these systems it will not help. The leadership has to come from all different places.

Kyle - I have seen so many protest leaders break in the protests to tell protestors to stop so they do not threaten the effectiveness of the protest by violence and lead to curfews and martial law because this is what a lot of our leaders really want and we can't give that to them. We have to peacefully protest and march. We are all grieving at this time and everyone grieves differently. I am happy to see a lot of white people stand up and stand by and protect our black and brown brothers and sisters. We all have to understand that if it turns violent, we are not helping the cause.

Shelley - People just want their voices to be heard. I was happy to see a diverse group of people join the protests. They are angry and just want someone to listen and for the leaders of North America to take action and make changes.

This episode took place on July 13th, 2020 on New Horizon Media Arts YouTube Channel

Episode - 38 - Mental Health Awareness and Wellness Workshop - Part 1

Background: Mental health is a very important matter and issue in Canada. Over the years many government organizations, corporations and educational institutions have taken measures to create awareness around the subjects of mental health. Today, mental health issues have substantially risen as a result of the lockdown arising out of the COVID-19 pandemic, as people lost their jobs, dealt financial trouble and lost their loved ones.

Panel discussion with eminent members of society - Fozia Murtaza, Suzan Hart, Tanya Ella Conlin, and Joseph Pitawanakwat Workshop Panelists background

Fozia Murtaza: Fozia is a Stress Prevention Strategist, Certified Facilitator for Wellness Recovery Action Plan (WRAP) Mental Health and Wellness Recovery workshops, Certified Life and Wellness Coach, Writer, Speaker, Ambassador for the Jamie Oliver Foundation (JOFR), member of the Durham Chapter of the Canadian Council of Muslim Women (CCMW), member of Happy Strong Family (HSF), member of Voices Against Stigma Everywhere (VASE), and member of the Malton Women Council (MWC)

Tanya Ella Conlin: Tanya is a community mental health worker, peer support specialist, and college professor. She has nearly 20 years of experience working in various areas of community mental health. For nearly 14 years, she has worked in the violence against women sector, while working with women in shelter at rape crisis centers through the family law process. She developed a number of training resources and offered support and training to other pers in the sector, across the province. In 2014, she joined the team at Durham Mental Health Services and has been working primarily in the crisis and peer programs since. Tanya is a certified RAP mental health and wellness recovery and safe management group facilitator and co-facilitates many groups. She is a passionate advocate for the people she works with and is dedicated to upholding the values and principles that Durham mental health services hold so dear.

Suzan Hart: Suzanne is a mindset mastery mentor, an author, inspirational speaker, and trainer. Suzanne has a background in psychology and over 15 years experience in family, individual, and group counselling. She helps leaders develop breakthrough strategies that reset their thinking. She operates at the intersection of personal leadership inclusive communication, and cultural competency. Her five step system allows leaders to overcome fear, doubt, and indecision, and powerfully respond when faced with a challenge. If you are tired of becoming paralyzed when confronted with the unknown of change, crisis, and chaos, it's time to learn the secret to unlocking the drive, passion, and focus needed to create massive results.

Joseph Pitawanakwat: Joseph is a holistic health educator who specializes in plant-based medicine. Joseph is an Ojibwe from Wiki Wemco. He is the founder and director of creators garden, an indigenous outdoor education and now online education-based business. His focus is on plant identification, sustainable harvesting, and teaching every one of their linguistic, historical, cultural, edible, ecological and medicinal significances through experiences. Joseph has developed a curriculum which he continuously lectures to a variety of organizations, including over 100 first nations communities, 20 universities and colleges across Canada and the United States. He is a Masters student in the MES program. He has learned from hundreds of traditional knowledge holders and uniquely blends that knowledge with an array of Western sciences. He is also working on his upcoming book, which focuses on ancient interpretive techniques, called the doctrine of signatures.

Episode - 38 - Mental Health Awareness and Wellness Workshop - Part 1

Fozia: According to a poll earlier this year by the Canadian Mental Health Association, 69% of Ontarians believe the province is headed for a serious mental health crisis, as it emerges from this pandemic and 77% say more mental health support will be necessary to help society. To help us understand the impact this pandemic has on the well-being of individuals and their families, we've invited Suzanne, Tanya, and Joseph to share with us. So, I want to pose a question to each of you, as you each work within a different field. How has social distancing impacted mental health for people? And we can start with Suzanne.

Suzanne: That is a great question, and I think one of the things that we want to look at in our society today is that we are a very busy interactive society and with that comes not much time to be with self, to be by yourself, and also to be with loved ones. So, what we're facing one is I think two things: a lot of people, not being accustomed to being left with themselves, and when we are not accustomed to being with themselves, we're not accustomed to being left with our thoughts, we're not accustomed to being left with our fears, we're not accustomed to being left with our emotions and we're not accustomed to not being distracted by other people and other things. So, I think for a lot of people, it's almost like I have too much time in my head by myself, thinking of things and I don't actually know how to manage my own thoughts. So, I think there's that piece. I think the other part that we're seeing people face is social distancing for many people feels like social isolation, right, and we also have families that have been so busy like two ships that are passing in the night, and suddenly we have people that aren't actually accustomed to being in relatedness, in the same place for extended periods of time and I think realizing that they don't actually have a relationship. And so, we're seeing increases in domestic violence, we're seeing increases in the divorce rates, separations, and then we're seeing increase with mental health, because I think what we're also seeing is emotions that have been suppressed, emotions that we've been too busy to deal with, emotions, things we have been too busy to think about, now people have to wait a lot of time with themselves and not able to actually manage a lot of the stuff that's happening. I think the last part is fear, you know, there's a lot of fear and we aren't accustomed to dealing with fear, which is a lot of what we do.

Fozia: Wow, that's a great perspective. Thank you for sharing that. And you make a great point. I think a lot of people are so caught up in the old norm that they're not aware of all of these things that they're experiencing and going through, so that probably has an impact as well. I want to give it over to Tanya because I think that a lot of what Suzanne said overlaps in probably what you're seeing with your clients as well.

Tanya: I'm going to answer that question by going back in time a little bit to a million ago in March and what happened to our clients is that they were going to groups, they were accessing services, they were accessing supports, and then one day, it all shut off. It was all taken away, and there wasn't a transition, there wasn't a warning, it just all stopped. And for many of the people that I work with, isolation is a very, very big problem already. A lot of them don't have a lot of family support, they may not have a lot of community support, there's so much stigma attached to mental health already that people really do rely on professional support and their peer connections within those professional supports. To have all that taken away so suddenly was very much like having the proverbial rug pulled out from underneath people. And what I found was people who had no access to their supports actually coping very well in the circumstances, but not able to see that they're coping very well in the circumstances. People I work with can be very hard on themselves, so if they struggle to cope, it is not an indicator that living under quarantine and with the uncertainty of COVID is hard, it is the conclusion that is often reached is that they aren't good at wellness, they aren't good at coping, and that's simply not the case. From my perspective, in my work, I have been able to see people really rise. We transformed our services very quickly onto an online format, which is not the same, but we are now into month six and I think that part of the mental health impact is that isolation continues, the zoom and the facetimes and all of the things that are taking place are great, but they're not the same. They don't necessarily get people out of the house, get people moving, and I think that we are now in a place where we have been doing this a really long time and we don't know what's going to happen. We're expecting this next wave of COVID, we're expecting flu season, and so okay, we're allowed out of our houses today, but are we going to be locked back up again tomorrow? And I think that means a lot of people are hesitant to return back to previous patterns, lifestyles, and even if they wanted to return back to their previous supports, a lot of places are still not offering in person support. So, it's really a challenge to get your needs met, and so what I have been seeing, and if I could just put a hopeful spin on it, is people who are really resourceful and doing what they can to get those needs met. I really enjoy the work that I do because I enjoy the people that I work with, and I admire them and respect them, the last 6 months have really given me so many more reasons to have that respect and to have that admiration, so on the one hand, it's been extraordinary, but on the other hand, I think people are doing the best that they can and they deserve a lot of credit. But I also think we're all suffering a collective post-traumatic stress. You can't stay in a heightened state of hypervigilance for six months and think that that's not going to have an impact long term.

Fozia: Absolutely. So much truth in what you said, Tanya. I can see Joseph really has something that he would like to add to that. Go ahead, sir.

Joseph: You guys are awesome, holy that is exactly what's up. Everything is pretty crazy. The only thing that I kind of would really like to say is that one of the really amazing things that I've been able to see because like before, I would travel to the community, take a whole bunch of families outside, and we would go and find all the plant medicine that we could find and yeah make all kinds of medicine. So, we're always doing the same thing, and March happens, and immediately everything has to be online. And like, I didn't even Skype with my Parents before all this, now my whole business has to be online, that was crazy! But we started and I got to be working in everybody's home now, it was actually a really good thing. One of my favourite, most important things that I have to establish and accomplish early on is ensuring that the participants are connecting to creation, they're connecting to the land, and then developing a relationship with it. We go out and pick medicine, and you need to be in a reciprocal relationship with each and every one of those plants, so that plant has gifts to give you and you have to give gifts back to it, mainly by way of seed collection and distribution, and helping with that whole cycle of reproduction. So, you're engaging in a relationship with all of these medicines, that is a really good way to connect somebody with something. So one of the coolest things that I saw in all of our online engagements is families going out together and establishing those relationships and those connections and receiving those gifts that those plants have to give them regarding their physical health and also just the fact that that connection and relationships were beginning and they were being fostered, there was significant impact on their mental health, their family's mental health. So for me, as a teacher, it ended up being one of the most beautiful things to see, and then to endorse and to motivate in all of our listeners and so one of the things I got everybody to do is to make a medicine map, because one of the things COVID does and is still doing, it forced everyone outside. Everyone was outside, it was crazy, maybe not everybody, but there were a lot more people outside. While we are outside, they created a medicine map of all of the medicine that they could find, all of the medicine that I taught them about, and they created a map. Now it's fall time, it's harvest time, and they're all engaging with it and they're being fulfilled as part of that process, and it ended up having a very positive impact on their mental health. And so we are big proponents of connecting to any green spaces, any land mass, the creation around you and observing the benefit in that.

Fozia: Thank you for that, I love that perspective of receiving but also giving back, and I think that is so necessary. I like how you each touched a little bit on the sort of being thrust into this situation, we've had to re-evaluate and really look at how we are spending our time and how we can utilize the type we've given, because right now, that's all we have – extra time, that we thought we didn't have. That takes me to my next question on how we would spend that time. When you're working with your clients, how important is it to create daily routines? Anyone who wants to go first.

Tanya: I can say something on that. I think what's really important is that we not put a lot of pressure on ourselves to be high achievers in this time, right, because I think that feeds into that notion of "well, I haven't learned a new language, and I haven't started playing guitar, and I haven't taken up woodworking, so I must be failing at COVID. I'm not baking bread everyday, I must be failing at COVID." So, while I think daily routine is super important, we know that is a big part of wellness, it's what we teach in RAP. Fozia and I have the opportunity to teach RAP together, it's a huge part of wellness, but I think when we talk about this, we want to make sure we're talking about daily routine and wellness, and not necessarily this idea that we have to suddenly become masters of this new talent that we've never attempted before. Because, there are a lot of people who have really said, is all I'm doing is what I need to do day in and day out, and I'm not doing what all these people are doing, again as though they're failing at wellness, and I'm looking at that and I'm like "that's what I'm doing too", right? Because I think that however we make it through the day is how we make it through the day and we don't need to learn Latin to make it through COVID successfully. But I think that daily routine is so important. I know that for myself, personally, I became the worst COVID snacker between March and probably yesterday, like in March and April, I was buying potato chips at the store, I don't do that, I will eat them if someone else has them, but I won't buy those. So, I think that when we don't have healthy daily maintenance plans, what we end up doing is resorting to unhealthy coping strategies, in my case potato chips, and we can get to a point where we're not getting dressed everyday, or we're getting dressed but we're actually just changing from one set of pajamas to another set of pajamas. It is so easy to get out of the routine of leaving your house, or brushing your hair, or having any sort of connection to anyone. So, I think that one of the things we teach in RAP is that when we start seeing signs that our wellness is in decline, the first thing we always talk about with our early warning signs, signs that things are breaking down, signs

that we're entering a crisis, the first thing we always tell people is to go back to your daily maintenance plan and look at what you're not doing. Because when we flip our days and nights, so that we're staying up all night, doing really unproductive things, like watching Netflix, and we're sleeping all day, or we're up too late and we're still getting up, or we're trying to balance working from home and having children at home learning, the degree of anxiety and panic that increased when the government released the curriculum in April, wow that really shot up. But, I think daily maintenance is absolutely critical, but again that doesn't necessarily mean that we have to put pressure on ourselves to be achievers in this time. But, I think that we can find new ways of connecting and new ways of adapting to this new reality of life that can be really positive, but we just have to walk that fine line, I think.

Fozia: Thank you for that and you're absolutely right, we do have to find that fine line. I know Suzanne has something to add, because I have worked with you and I know that daily routines for you are a ritual, so can you elaborate a little bit on that?

Suzanne: Absolutely. I think one of the things I want to start with as we're talking about mental health, I think we're talking about mental health for everyone. For anyone listening, I don't want someone to exclude themselves from this conversation because they think, "well I don't have a mental health issue". Mental health is the looking at how we are all coping with change, stress, all those different things, so I think that as COVID is evolving, it is challenging everyone's mental health, because whenever we are faced with change, and particularly change that we didn't choose, it challenges our sense of self, it challenges our mental health, it challenges our coping mechanisms and it challenges what we routinely do and for those who don't have routines, it often creates a lot more chaos in your life. For me, one of the key things about rituals and routines, I often refer to it as home base, it is home base and whatever it is for you, anyone who works with me I recommend they have a morning routine, and a routine to close off their day, and they actually build a schedule that schedules what they want to do in the day, and that's home base. Why homebase is so key at this time, is as Tanya says, when you move away from it, you know you're gone, whereas if you don't have it, you tend to drift and you don't actually know what you're supposed to come back to. So, the beautiful thing about having a ritual and routine, is that it gives you a grounding foundation so that when emotions rise and things seem challenging and chaotic, it becomes your home base where you can go back and say "this is what grounds me", so that's the first thing. I think the second thing that is really cool about this whole process is that I have the two bookends, morning routine, evening routine, but in the middle of that, where I tell people three goals: they don't have to be rocket science, they could be "I'm going to go for a walk today, I'm going to get this project done today, I'm going to get something else today", and what it does is one, it gives us focus, but it also gives us a sense of success. For me, even if it is "I made my bed, I went for a long walk", our mind loves success. A mind that is trained to celebrate success will go looking for success. So, another part of having a ritual and routine is actually teaching yourself to one, create opportunities for success and create opportunities to celebrate your success, and then move from that place into the next day. And what that does for people is when we're in situations where days can flow into weeks, and weeks can flow into months, and you're blinking and your eyes are going "what happened? It was Monday, now it's Sunday. What happened in between?" it gives opportunities to create natural breaks, there's a natural break at the beginning and end of the day. The problem is when we're home and in isolation and all of these different things, those natural breaks aren't as evident, because we're not going out to work and coming home, so ritual and routine also highlights those natural breaks and allows you to create your own successes and your own focus throughout the day.

Fozia: I love that, such a great way to look at it. I hear what both of you are saying, even in a time of such uncertainty and chaos, having routines set up for ourselves gives us that sense of being in control somewhat, in a situation that is obviously out of our control. I want to switch it over to Joseph, I'm going to ask you a question based on what Suzanne said, and this brings it to managing our mental health as a daily and not just if someone is experiencing mental illness. So, what roles do you find that indigenous remedies play in aiding and managing our mental health on a daily basis?

Thanks for watching us and we will be back next week, same time, with part 2 of this episode.

This episode took place on October 4th, 2020 on New Horizon Media Arts YouTube Channel

Episode - 39 - Mental Health Awareness and Wellness Workshop - Part 2

Fozia: I'm going to ask you a question, Joseph, based on what Suzan said, and this brings it to managing our mental health as a daily, not just if someone is experiencing mental illness. So what roles do you find Joseph that indigenous remedies play in aiding and managing our mental health on a daily basis?

Joseph: Yeah, so one of the things that I saw that happens immediately is now, out of all of the programs that we offer as a business, like on metabolism, on women's health, on addictions, on arthritis, out of everything that we do, absolutely I'll give everyone a big laundry list, march only mental health. Now everyone only wants to look at or to understand more about medicines – plant medicines role in managing and helping to manage mental health. There's a few key ones, so we created and have been delivering this program for about four years now, so I don't know – all over the place, it's been crazy. Over the last four years, we have been able to sort of hone in on the most impactful because we offer experiences, we give people the medicine we don't like, we try not to just teach about it and walk away. We give people the medicine there, that day, and I ask for a cross-section of people who consider themselves mentally healthy to those in really bad places, at all different ages and those who work at all different capacities, bring them all – a cross section of everybody and we'll all record our impact or what this medicine is doing to me. So, it's what we do, it ends up being pretty rigorous. Of course, not with the rigor of studying or something like this, but there is rigor behind it, whether the participants know it or not. Over the past four years, yeah, we've been able to hone in on what is the most impactful. So there's two things that I want to say. Number one is the most impactful medicine that we could provide for somebody regarding their mental health. It's actually really funny because it's not considered a mental health medicine. It's medicine for your gut, it's for your intestine, it's a plant we call (**), it's sweet fern, comptonia peregrina and we make tea and so when we're looking at our physical health, we're looking at our body, the largest source of inflammation, of chronic low- grade levels of inflammation is coming from our gut and so because like the open junction and things that we call leaky gut, one of the ways that your body can sort of seal your intestines from bacterias and proteins going out into your body, creating this huge inflammatory response, your intestines can seal this with an amino acid called glutamine, or we will call mucin. That's what that medicine will work with – re-establishing and creating more mucin to seal that barrier in your intestines and remove the largest source of inflammation. So we just sort of watched that happen organically, it happened naturally, where we were able to see that the medicine that seems to have the largest impact on people's mental health long-term is medicine for inflammation and then to look into literature and identify a lot of issues regarding anxiety and depression being largely uncontrolled or unmanageable because of excessive amounts of inflammation. So that just sort of happened as a byproduct on the side and so we had a lot of fun with that. The main medicine that we sort of offer, the main plant that we offer is, it's called rican leaves. It is a sweet flag, of course calamus or americanus, and that one is one of my favourites. So yeah, aside from the whole inflammation and gaining control within that, the medicine that works specifically with our mental health is going to be this plant that we call sweet flag or chorus calamus americanus, it grows all over the place, it's really common. Generally, we only use the roots, but when we use the leaves, this is how we help with chieftains of mental health. We look at anxiety and depression, and the way that we explain this, it's my absolute favourite to use in high schools because high schools are rough, it's totally different. I was only in high schools a couple years ago, now it's crazy. I can't even imagine going through that. It's my favourite to use there, because we notice the impact so fast. When I go into a high school, we'll make the tea and we'll all just enjoy this. It's really delicious, tastes like lemongrass. You can even use it in your cooking this way, perfume your rice and then your medicine is within your food, just the way that it was supposed to be anyway. Anyway, you have two parts to your nervous system, you have your sympathetic nervous system and your parasympathetic nervous system, and they sort of pendulate between one another. Your sympathetic nervous system is your stress response, it's your survival mode, it's when something happens and you have to deal with it. Your parasympathetic is relaxing and sleeping, calming down, lowering your heart rate, lowering your blood pressure. They go back and forth between each other, throughout the day, something happens and we deal with it, and we calm down, and then something else happens, and they go back and forth and back and forth. One of the things that happens when we're not a part of a culture or a part of a system that allows us to be able to, it's a learned strategy to be able to be able to learn how to manage that pendulation and so it's experts like Suzan and Tanya that are there to teach us how to keep this pendulating properly, to be able to understand how this works. But what happens, the role that medicine plays in the management of mental health is when we receive a trauma and we go survival mode and we go sympathetic, and your parasympathetic cannot do its job, it can't pull you back all the way, it can't fully relax you and fully lower your heart rate, it can't give you control over your own breath and so what happens is you stay slightly elevated, slightly sympathetic, slightly survival mode, slightly stressed out. And the longer you stay there, the more opportunity that will establish itself as chemistry and establish itself as a new normal. And when that's your new normal, slightly stressed out all the time, it's easier for triggers to happen and a trigger happens, another trauma happens, and you go sympathetic and we're not engaging or not a part of these systems that teach us how to manage this pendulation, so your parasympathetic can't pull you again all the way. And then that will turn into a new normal, and this one will turn into a new normal, and then this one, and so you create or you establish this ladder of chemistry or this ladder of new normal, until you're just rocking sympathetic all the time. And we look at this as anxiety, and this as depression, and the longer you stay in that state, this will manifest itself in a physical form that we will call PTSD. So, medicine's role is to bypass this, it's to take that chemical ladder and those physical representations and remove it. And so what this medicine does, there's a surgery that you could do, that's called a stellar ganglion block for PTSD to help manage PTSD and when pharmaceutical industry, pharmaceutical company looks into the natural world to identify a plant component that is able to establish the same thing, the number one candidate is and has been for like 30 years, sweet flag, of course calamus americanus, they've been using our medicine to try to create a drug, and it has been unsuccessful for the past 30 years. The surgery has been being done since the 20s, what they're able to identify is this medicine creates a bypass mechanism around the stellar ganglion rather than paralyzing it, like what the surgery does is it establishes a bypass mechanism, bypassing all of this chemistry that has been created to then allow that parasympathetic action, to allow you to suddenly have control over your heart rate, to have control over your breath, to be able to calm down, to be able to relax, to be able to sleeps, and so when we spend a couple of days inside of a high school, the very next day, sometimes even by the end of the day, students that have red faces, such high blood pressure and just on edge all the time, but even sometimes by the end of the day, they already notice that there's something different that's happening. And then they go home and they sleep 12 hours and then they come back to school the next day with this resilience, that's one of my favourite things, I love going to high schools just for that, and observing the impact that that medicine can have. But really, medicine plays an important role, but its that council, it's that system that is there to give us the support we need to continue the pendulation that is the longevity of mental health adaptation and resilience and strength within that system. That's where it is, in those supports, and so that's why Suzan, Tanya, they're the ones doing the real work, this medicine is just able to give you the ability to feel what it feels like to have normal function. It's up to the individual to maintain that normal function.

Suzanne: If I could add, what Joseph is saying is so profound and so important because it speaks to two key things that we don't do in our north American society. One is we don't eat foods that promote great mental health or promote health. So you know one of the biggest things, I'm not going to name any companies, but the food that's on the rise are all the foods that create inflammation in the body which wreaks havoc on our system. We are designed to eat processed foods and fast foods, and we're getting further and further away from the earth, which means more challenges for our mental health. The second thing is we are a society that is conditioned to suppress our emotions, right – deal with that later, be strong, don't talk about that, don't seek help, and the tougher you are and the more tough exterior you have, and the less you deal with your emotions, seems to be the more we're rewarded in society. We combine those two together, and now you have a situation when people are left alone, that's what they know, and so you see now, you see people "i'm an emotional eater", well an emotional eater is the answer to pushing down your emotions and eating them. I'm blowing up, well anger is normal, anger is a way of "I haven't dealt with the emotion", and maybe the emotion is not anger but it's showing up as anger. Depression is suppressed emotions, we have all these things, so our answer is to drug it or suppress it, which are neither working, and so we're in this cycle and then you add something like COVID on top of that, and you have people at heightened states of emotions, heightened states of fear, heightened states of anxiety, and no coping mechanisms because they're natural in how we survive. And so what we're really talking about is, like when you did this, I was like oh my gosh that's so good. When it doesn't come back here, how you get it back here is emotional awareness. It's an awareness of your emotions and then implementing coping appeals that allow things to come back to that place. Well we are not conditioned to be aware of what's going on emotionally and mentally, so that we can actually learn to do the work, so that we can learn to get back into this place of rest. We're not even conditioned to get enough sleep, so our natural society is doing all the things that are contrary to mental health, but yet having mental health, it doesn't work.

Fozia: Beautifully said, I love that piece. And what I'm hearing from both of you is that we've moved away from that mindfulness and really managing our mindset. And because of that disconnect, that we are open to all of these other things that are causing chaos internally and externally for us, and that was what my next question was going to be: what's the connection in all of this, between mindset and mental health, and I think you guys have both touched on that. Tanya, I know that you do a lot of work with people with mindfulness, so did you want to add a piece to this?

Tanya: I think the way you think about things changes what happens to you, in a sense. That we can focus on things being unfair or uncalled for, and oftentimes, things are unfair and uncalled for, and we often don't get what we deserve, and there are often people who get things that they haven't earned. But, we can focus there, but that is not a forward focus. That is not a focus that is going to have our momentum in a forward direction, toward our wellness, toward our goals, and I think when we choose to focus instead on "what responsibility can I take in this situation", responsibility isn't a blame, it's not about saying "I made this mess, so I have to clean it up," but it's about looking at things and going, "I am the most qualified to fix this", and fixing it, regardless of who actually did the breaking. And I think that when we really go through life looking for the things that we can have responsibility over, we're looking for things that we're also looking for things that we can have control over, actions that we can take that take into account our resources, our knowledge, our supports, our abilities in that particular moment in time, cause that changes. So, all of those things are quite variable, and I think that when we go through life asking the question of "does this advance our health or wellness, or doesn't it", then we're moving through life in a more mindful way. And we're able to do things like pick our battles, choose food that nurtures our bodies, fuels our bodies. I always think of our nutrition like the different fluids in a car. If you try to run a car without oil, you're going to be in for a very big surprise. And again, when it comes down to that daily maintenance and daily routine, when people call our crisis line and they're having that super resistant crisis, where they just can't come down, and you say to them, "what have you eaten today", "nothing". "What have you had to drink today that didn't have alcohol or caffeine today?", "well I've had six coffees". "When was the last time you slept, when was the last time you showered?" A lot of times, people think that you don't even want to listen to me, that's so sensitive. No, what I want you to do is give your body what it needs to control its crisis right now. And oftentimes, we neglect the most, the easiest things we can change. We can go have a glass of water, we can go and put minerals, nutrients, proteins, healthy fats in our bodies. We can do things to increase the amount of rest we have. I'm like the most notorious insomniac you will meet in your life, I have all of the sleep disorders right here. So, I understand how hard that can be and how you have to sometimes think of rest differently and expand our definition of that. What do we need to do to rejuvenate ourselves? Does that mean being in nature and communicating in nature? Fozia, I think that was you that said you like to stand in the grass – I think that if we can go through life asking that question, "Does this enhance my wellness, or does it take away from my wellness", and if it takes away from our wellness, why are we even doing it? What's the motivation here? And if we're doing it because someone else wants us to, or to avoid someone else getting angry at us, or to avoid someone else's emotions, we really need to think about that.

Fozia: Very well said, I love how you put the responsibility back to ourselves, and that's really empowering. I just want to give Suzan a moment to add to this, because I know this is your piece, because you are the mindset master mentor. If you want to add something right there, because I know Tanya is speaking your truth now.

Suzanne: She is so speaking my truth, and Tanya thank you so much, so well said. And I think one of the things when I've been looking at what's occurring during these past six months, there are three types of people, and the three types will also determine their state of mental health. There's been the group of people that you watch that are watching everything on the news, they're watching everything negative, they're watching all this stuff, and they're angry at everything outside of themselves. And so, they're like, when are the politicians going to tell us this, did you notice that the politicians didn't do this, did you know that the hospitals didn't do this, and what they're not looking at is, they are feeling out of control and they are looking for someone to help them regain a sense of control. But, the challenge is they're looking outside of themselves. But when you do that, all you do is play the waiting game, for someone else to make change so that you can experience change that's beneficial to you. So we have a lot of society that's doing that, and the anxiety and anger is rising. Then you have the other group of people, and Tanya you alluded to this at the beginning as well, is "I'm just going to wait for this to be over and I'm going to bake, I'm going to create a new habit, hobby, I'm going to this and that" and while that is functional in the moment, it's also another way to avoid what's going on. So, there's those that focus on every detail, there are those who have their head in the sand and avoid, but avoiding doesn't mean the emotions go away. Avoiding isn't coping, avoiding is still avoiding. So you're going to feel that, how long can we wait it out, there's going to be a point where the wait is too long because resources may run out, things may happen, so there's a group that's avoiding, and that's still not taking responsibility. And then there's a third group who are really going, first thing they're doing, "I need to accept what's happening", and I'm using the word intentionally. Once they've accepted it, they do exactly what Tanya is saying – "What can I take responsibility for, what do I have the ability to do in order to recreate a sense of feeling in control?" Because that's what we're missing for many people, the sense of feeling in control. The reality is we were never in control at all anyway, right, things were predictable, but now things aren't predictable and we're trying to regain a sense of control. But what you always have control over is what you choose to believe, how you choose to respond, how you choose to look at things, what you choose to influence you, and that's the place where change can happen. So you might say that I'm going to turn off the TV because it's influencing me negatively, I'm not going to communicate with people who are not giving me things that are empowering because it's influencing me negatively. Then you're able to ask yourself, "I'm managing my influences, how can respond right now, what are things I can do, what routines can I put in place to help me feel in control of the things that I can't manage, that are no longer predictable? What can I do to at least make my environment a little more predictable?" Now, people are in a place where, I call it "living in the face of their emotions", they're experiencing emotions, making clear choices, but they're also taking back charge. Because, as Tanya is saying, the one thing we have 100% responsibility for is ourselves, but it's also the one thing we have 100% control over, is our choices, not anyone else's. So to sit in that place and I go, ask yourself, "How can I be the hero in my life?", versus sitting in a place of victim, how can I be my own hero?

Fozia: Wow, I love that – "how can I be my own hero in my life?" and that's a great way to look at it. I just realized we're coming to the top of the hour. The time has gone by so quickly. So as we come to a close, I want to ask each of you if you could leave the viewers with a final word with what they can do to support their mental health and their self-care. Just a quick final word. Who wants to go first?

Tanya: I was the kid in school who couldn't let a question go unanswered in class. If you notice that when you don't designate a question in a certain direction, I can't help myself. I think that one of the things we have to realize is that this is a hard situation. We are not struggling because we are bad cops or terrible at wellness. We are struggling because this is hard. If you guys will indulge with me, I would like to share my marathon analogy, Fozia has heard this seven million times and I apologize to her. It's inspired by the Women's Marathon at the Rio Olympics four years ago, one of the female Olympians was a medal winner, took two steps over the finish line and collapsed. But did she collapse because she was a bad runner? Because that's what our clients say to themselves, that they're struggling not because things are hard, but because they're bad at coping. She took two steps over that finish line and collapsed because marathons in July in Rio are hard. She is an Olympic class athlete and she is going to run again, probably within a couple of days of that finish line, and she is going to continue to do great things. She's an amazing runner, she just finished 42.2 km. She hasn't collapsed because she's a bad runner, it's because it's hard. There are people puking in the bushes. The first aid tent is full, because marathons in July are hard. We are all at the finish line, we're probably not at the finish line actually, we're at the water station in a marathon, going "how do we keep going?" But we can keep going, because we've been going. We've made it this far. It's so important to recognize that we do have coping skills, we do have coping strategies, it's okay to reach out and supplement that with health. We sometimes do have to look at or consider the fact that the support within our friends and family circles may not be qualified to provide us with the support we need, and to reach out to more professional types of supports, or different kinds of support, and recognize that that's okay. It doesn't mean we failed. We are marathon runners in July! Puking isn't a sign that we're bad at it, it's a sign that it is hard, and that's okay.

Fozia: Awesome, thank you for that. Suzan, final word for our viewers?

Suzanne: I think what I would say is that look for the blessing. And why I say that is that there's a saying that what you focus on, you find. If you focus on how hard this is, and we will have moments where we will experience hardship, you will find that this is hard the whole time. If you focus on how unfair this is, you will find that it is unfair. But if you choose to focus on, "what's the blessing in this, what's the learning, what's the opportunity for me to grow, what's the opportunity for me to transform?" Joseph said it was the opportunity for his business to get online and he's probably touching way more lives than he had when he was travelling. What's the blessing? And when you start looking for the business, remember what you focus on, you always find. Well, the blessing will give you opportunities to become more, it'll give you opportunities to grow, give you opportunities to say, "I needed more family time, I needed to slow down, sleep more, I needed time alone." What is the blessing? And when you find it, nurture it, water it, allow it to grow, and then look for another blessing.

Fozia: Awesome, thank you so much for that. So true – find the blessing, that's a great share and great message for everyone. Joseph, final words to our viewers?

Joseph: One of the things I keep thinking about every time these guys are talking, I keep thinking one time I was out getting medicine and we were getting arthritis medicines, and I was with one of the teachers I learned from, and he said, "I'll go to pick medicine". And so I went that way, and we came back, and all of his trees were really awful looking. Mine looked beautiful, perfect, and he looked awful, and I thought, "how come you're getting all those horrible looking trees?" and he said, "these are the ones you have to get, these are the ones that are stronger medicine." And that just bugged me real bad, he's my teacher, I want to understand everything he's saying, so I take it as an opportunity to learn, what is he talking about? And every time we'd go out and pick medicine, he's always finding all of these plants that are struggling, like they're just hanging on, and so one of the things that I was able to learn from that was the more stress that a plant has had to overcome, the stronger it is. When a fungus tries to attack a plant, the plant has to activate its immune system and kill that fungus with what we call medicine. So, the more fungus that's attacking it, the more response that that plant has to have.

So when you go to pick medicine, you always find the plants that have overcome the most amount of stress, the most moose lipped, scumming and eating all of the branches, the most rabbits nibbling on it, the more mites boring into it, the more fungus attacking it, those are all signs that this plant is going to be stronger medicine. And for some of them, they can be almost 60 times stronger, if you find a plant that has been through it, versus a beautiful little plant that never dealt with anything its whole life. So, it can be almost 60 times more active, so it's the same thing with us. When we exercise, when we go to the gym, nobody goes to the gym now, but when you go to the gym and you're lifting a dumbbell, you're stressing out that bicep. The more stress you apply to that muscle, the bigger and stronger that it's going to be. And the same thing – you go for a run, you're stressing out your cardiovascular system. The more runs you go on, the faster and further you're going to be able to run. You're going to be adapting to that stress. So, we look for it in medicine but its pretty analogous to the things that we have to deal with. And understanding that mental health is an important aspect as to who we are as people, and it needs to be fostered and nurtured in the same way as our physical, spiritual, emotional health. All these things have to be working together, they're all parts of our being. The more stress, stress is always an opportunity for growth, a signal for growth, an opportunity for change, and the more of those that we have, the more opportunity we have to get stronger. So, identifying that perspective is really nice. That's been a lot of the things that some of the participants in our programming have been able to see. When they go out, they're able to just identify and relate so much more with the medicine that they're picking, because maybe they've been through it all too. And to have that little shift inside them, when we go out and get medicine like this, we get outside and we have those experiences of those relationships, it's really fun to be able to see and so these guys, they're the ones that know how to overcome those stresses. They're the masters in giving us the tools that we need to get this system stronger, to see this as an opportunity for growth, an opportunity for change, to be exposed like experts like Suzan and Tanya, to be able to give you the tools you need to work that system out and get it stronger. It's really neat to be able to be here with these gals.

Fozia: Thank you so much for that, Joseph. I just love the final thoughts that you guys are leaving our viewers with, and so true – we will come out of this stronger. This has been such a great discussion, I want to thank each of you for taking the time to speak with us today, and for our viewers that are interested in getting in touch with any of our panelists, you can do this by contacting us here at New Horizons Media Arts. Thank you again guys, enjoy the rest of your day.

This episode took place on October 24th, 2020 on New Horizon Media Arts YouTube Channel

Editor's Biography

Yashaswi Vig: Yashaswi is a final year Undergraduate Finance student at Concordia University. She started her writing career by getting involved in the student associations in University. She has dedicated a major part of her University career towards adding value to student life and has contributed as a writer and published business articles on topics and issues trending in the business industry to enable students to become more knowledgeable.

She is a self-driven, result oriented and talented individual who is very hard working and is striving towards building a successful career in the field of Finance and Law.

Priya Annapurni: Priya, through a career spanning over two decades, has worked in several different fields. Her career journey began during her undergraduate education when she started working with rural artisans, helping them design and market traditional fabric and garments. Following this experience, Priya established and ran a successful garment business and later became a global consultant for a multinational CAD/CAM company and a member of the Faculty at NIFT, New Delhi. Thereafter, she made a career shift into HR and has worked in this field since. In her fifteen years of experience, she has been employed in a number of organizations across three countries. Her most recent role was that of a Global HR Business Partner with one of the top five Chemical companies in the world, SABIC.

Priya is a resilient professional who has reinvented herself multiple times, starting each career journey from scratch and excelling within that field. She is deeply passionate about enabling, empowering, and supporting people from all walks of life in maximizing their potential. After collaborating with diverse groups and working in various countries, Priya truly believes that each individual brings a unique knowledge base, skillset, and perspective, all of which are critical to the overall success of any initiate, organization, or community.

Co- Author's Biography

Shirin Ariff: Shirin is an Inspirational Speaker, Award Winning 5xInternational Bestselling Author, a Resiliency Coach for Women and a proud single mother of 4 beautiful children. Shirin speaks to professional association members about how to be true to themselves; to find their own North Star as a guide in their professional and personal lives.

Shirin is on a mission to empower and transform women who are victims of any kind of abuse. She's been there. Her own story of dramatic ups and downs and her remarkable journey of resilience which involved coming to Canada, and then becoming a single mother, surviving cancer and struggling with facial paralysis, inspires others with the wisdom and strength she gained along the way.

Shirin is passionate about and committed to the idea of empowering women to find dignity and freedom in their lives.

Shirin received the International Women Achievers Award 2020 as a Woman of Purpose Spiritual Writer/Composer Halo Award for 2020

Shirin received the Literary Titan Award for her meditative poetry book, "Keepsake". Shirin is a Guinness Book of Record Holder for 2020.

Lata Gullapall: Lata is an investment banker who specializes in Mergers and Acquisition and has travelled and worked in South Asia, Russia and the U.K.

She advises companies on financial restructure and capital raising. She has designed products for raising capital and have set up and run startup companies, devising strategy and funding for them.

She is also an author, with published stories to excellent reviews and currently working on two book writing projects.

She has achieved an education in corporate law, financial strategy, taxation and economics, among others. She has an MBA from INSEAD in France and is a chartered secretary, and chartered financial analyst (I).

She is also involved with NGOs in the U.K. and in India that are focused primarily on and are involved in child protection, education for the girl child and orphaned children.

References

Episode 1- htttps://www.youtube.com/watch?v=wgH1CRgFSdI&t=331s
Episode 5- htttps://www.youtube.com/watch?v=bFJNC1cVT4Y
Episode 8- htttps://www.youtube.com/watch?v=jiFIZfUvY7w
Episode 9- https://www.youtube.com/watch?v=hypCQkIPVGQ
Episode 11- https://www.youtube.com/watch?v=qGroZw5UVQs
Episode 12- https://www.youtube.com/watch?v=OKZsPPbGKKo
Episode 13- https://www.youtube.com/watch?v=5yKgKCwQlXQ
Episode 14- https://www.youtube.com/watch?v=MjN58ACwR14
Episode 15- https://www.youtube.com/watch?v=Czx-9u0PkXE
Episode 18- https://www.youtube.com/watch?v=dyeNQ9SheZs
Episode 19- https://www.youtube.com/watch?v=Am6d5BCv3CI
Episode 20- https://www.youtube.com/watch?v=Qk0WDbiEHa4
Episode 21- https://www.youtube.com/watch?v=thBCRw3tdAM
Episode 24- https://www.youtube.com/watch?v=o_vBZdqcIT0
Episode 25- https://www.youtube.com/watch?v=7EX0H6qJ9aI
Episode 26- https://www.youtube.com/watch?v=I3d14I3kUMU
Episode 27- https://www.youtube.com/watch?v=ra7to_u6LdU&t=112s
Episode 28- https://www.youtube.com/watch?v=JKJAIYqFJNs
Episode 30- https://www.youtube.com/watch?v=2mJQk_ZKVZU
Episode 31- https://www.youtube.com/watch?v=9KlJfCx0q60&t=857s
Episode 32- https://www.youtube.com/watch?v=0zBGlcwe65Q
Episode 34- https://www.youtube.com/watch?v=cmRV6yG6m7Y
Episode 36- https://www.youtube.com/watch?v=B3xdcMDbSpI
Episode 38- https://www.youtube.com/watch?v=QpfRmhteoDg&t=189s
Episode 39- https://www.youtube.com/watch?v=1qM8uikIC8s
Episode 40- https://www.youtube.com/watch?v=BDhAn2RwMco&t=519s
Episode 41- https://www.youtube.com/watch?v=sROoNzmeUZw

Authors

1. Shirin Ariff
2. Abdullah Zakaria
3. Sujay Jha
4. Sandeep Bose
5. Shelley Jarrett
6. Cheryl Jairaj
7. Ranjan Bakshi
8. Seemant K Singh
9. Meeta Khanna
10. Roger Caesar
11. Lata Gullapalli
12. Sean C Dwyer
13. Ujjwal Roy Chowdhuri
14. Karan Sehmbi
15. Steve Elliot
16. Hari Iyer
17. Jay Wijesundara
18. Asis Sethi
19. Fozia Murtaza
20. Suzan Hart
21. Tanya Ella Conlin
22. Joseph Pitawanakwat
23. Melanie Pereira

CPSIA information can be obtained
at www.ICGtesting.com
Printed in the USA
BVHW092003220321
602948BV00002B/3